# SUPER BASIC
# ADULTING

## What Everyone Expects You to Already Know About Being a Mature, Goal-Setting, Financially Planned, and Career-Focused Adult

*by*

# PAUL D. PANTERA

Panterax Ltd

ISBN: Paperback- 978-1-957442-16-7
ISBN: Hardcover- 978-1-957442-17-4
ISBN: eBook-      978-1-957442-24-2

# Dedication

This book is inspired by and dedicated to my son, Jelani, in hopes of providing some tools in his journey into adulthood. No matter if you read this immediately, 10, or 20 years from now the information here can assist in guiding, affirming, or transforming your life. My own life has been changed for the better often by picking up a book I've walked by for years before opening it up. Often, we need to be ready for the information before we can see it, receive it, and believe it.

# Gratitude

I am eternally grateful to the team that worked with me to bring this work to life: Jack Bonanza, Manda Lorain, Ravi Ramgati, and Ileana Blanco.

I am forever grateful to my Great Uncle Robert Carey, who was instrumental in helping me develop self-awareness while in college so that eventually, I could ask myself questions to direct my life where I desired.

I am deeply grateful for the continued love and support of my wife, Yolanda, who represents a great reward for my developing into a mature adult. 'Whoso findeth a wife findeth a good thing, and obtaineth favour of the Lord.' – *The Bible Proverbs 18:22*

# PANTERAX

Sign up for our newsletter and
receive a FREE ebook of puzzles at:

## http://pantheria.net

# Table of Contents

# Introduction

Have you ever seen one of those memes about school never teaching you how to do taxes? That's what this book is about.

Well…we won't be talking about taxes really (at least, not a lot). Neither will we be talking about how the mitochondria is the powerhouse of the cell.

No, here, we're actually going to talk about how people *find out* about doing their taxes.

We're going to talk about adulting: the process of becoming an adult and coming to terms with our place in the world as an adult.

You see, many people don't simply become adults; they actually remain teenagers, until they wake up one day and realize they should *be* adults. What ensues is a mad scramble to figure out what taxes are and how far behind they are in paying them, the arrival of panic as they realize they are alone and need to survive, as well as some harsh lessons as they come to realize they're the only 28-year-old in a club full of college freshmen — and they have work tomorrow.

You see, one of the great tragedies of our age is that we often grow up so sheltered. Our parents shelter us. Our high school friends shelter us. College creates a bubble that *looks* like adulthood, but is softened with the same safety netting as a school (dormitories, classes, tests, student discounts, etc.), ultimately sheltering us. Even more so, many of the jobs you can find after college have entry-level positions that are designed to make the transition from college to the office smooth, often with a few training programs and required social events every Friday, giving you a nice safety bubble that will probably not pop until you're in your late 20s. Chances are good that if you are reading this, you've been living an incredibly sheltered life.

What all this means is that if you do something dumb in college, you'll likely get a disciplinary hearing—not a jail cell. I'm not advocating that people should be thrown in jail to "teach 'em' a lesson," I'm just simply saying that much of the coldness adult life brings is often kept away from most people for a long time.

No one is ever going to sit you down and say: "You're an adult now." It's not something that magically happens as soon as you turn 18 or 21, get a degree, or find a flat. It's something that dawns on you when you look around and realize you *need* to adult.

This isn't right. It's often too late when this happens, and it tends to cause a bit of a mental health crisis for many people.

For some people, this realization is not an issue; they have been adulting since they were teens, and never noticed it. For others, they'll never notice...they'll simply go from college to a soft job, find a wealthy fiancé, and only realize they should have been adults when their kids hate them, and their partner wants a divorce at 48.

For most, it will happen one day in their mid-20s when they realize no one is looking after them. At this point it becomes a mad scramble to either build yourself up, survive, or fall into poverty.

I write this book because I want to stop you from falling. The school doesn't need to teach us taxes. It needs to teach people the reality of the world — how cruel it can be, and what we need to do to pull through and live a happy life.

It needs to teach us values.

It needs to give us practical solutions to real-world problems we'll all one day face.

Sadly, no one is making any memes on this, so I took it upon myself to translate some of what I've learned about life into a book that I hope can help you as you get ready to leave the nest. This book was designed to tie into a life planner I made called *Pantheria Life Log*, and contains a few exercises derived from that text. If you really want to master the skills I discuss here and apply them practically, I recommend checking out the *Pantheria Life Log* on Amazon—a diary I made to help people track their progress in life and constantly set and gain goals.

The Pantheria Life Log is available in Black, Navy Blue, and Purple.

In this book, my aim is not only to give you some good advice that you can use to always stand on your two feet and keep going, but to orient you to an understanding of what the world requires you to do/know, as well as give you some practical tips with which to tackle some uniquely adult problems.

Oh, and on a final note: If you feel this book is what you needed, or it helps you at all, please help me out and leave a positive review on Amazon. People will often undergo a great deal of effort to complain, yet seldom will bother opening their browser to say something nice. If you do this, it can help spread this book to others and assist me greatly in promoting something I am quite passionate about, and put a great deal of effort into.

# ASKING
# THE RIGHT QUESTIONS

To understand what it means to be an "adult," you must understand what it means to be a person. Now, that statement alone can quickly escalate and branch this chapter into a variety of philosophical discussions on the "meaning of life," "the search for value," "consciousness," or what it means to "love." But no...I will do us all a favor by avoiding this approach and giving you a simple—yet helpful—observation I made about people that you can use to guide yourself far in life.

Please don't misunderstand, questions on the "meaning of life" are central to any human's journey through life, but they are reserved for each of us to discover on our own. Although I will occasionally be touching on such high topics from time to time, it will never be done for the sake of "lecturing" you, but rather for you to have things to think about as you seek to find your own answers. For the most part, this book is simply written to help you plant your feet on the ground as you brace to deal with life.

Now...to turn back to the aforementioned observation: What does it mean to be a "person"?

Well, for most people, it will boil down to their own patterns. You see, all people on earth have patterns and behaviors that they repeat and re-perform again, and again, indefinitely for the rest of their lives until they pass away. We simply learn a series of behaviors during our youth, and if they don't hurt us, we keep doing them again and again; we're still alive, so they must be of some value. There is nothing wrong with this; our minds are wired to do so for the sake of survival. After all, if you do the same thing over and over again, then you are doing something that hasn't resulted in death.

You'll be doing the things that don't hurt you.

The issue, however, is that most worthwhile things in life hurt before they begin to fulfill us.

In addition, very often we get hurt as children due to bad luck, when a repetition of behaviors would have actually been okay 95% of the time otherwise.

That's the name of the game, really...we do what we know, because what we know is safe. Now the issue is this. Just because our patterns have been keeping us alive, even happy, doesn't mean they are inherently good for us. What's more, the patterns become so ingrained in us that we often don't even know they are there; they become habits we simply notice in hindsight. These habits apply not only to the things we do, but the way we feel and navigate those feelings. Indeed, there are emotional habits, also, some of which are very unhealthy.

For example, you may have formed the habit in your life of dealing with the stress of homework or a test by "escaping." For most, this means video games or messing around with friends; for the unfortunate, it will mean drugs. In order to conquer these habits, you must first identify that they are there.

As you continue to read this book, I intend to take you on a journey of learning how to identify your habits—your patterns—and how to change them for the better. This is *not* an easy thing. Quite the contrary—as we go down this road you will soon discover that changing even one habit will be incredibly difficult. You may even trick yourself into thinking it's impossible. The reason why is because your brain will be fighting you every step of the way. After all, why change a habit if it's been "working"? Surely that isn't safe?

You see, the brain evolved in a world where doing something different means getting eaten by a tiger or beaten by the tribe's elder. For the sake of your own safety, rather do the drugs and play video games. Keep your head down and avoid doing "new" things, like doing the "new" homework and talking with "new" friends.

That is the nature of the monster we will be slaying.

Yet if you wish to become a functional adult, you must face it, nonetheless. For many, this will be done accidentally through a series of harsh and painful memories as they go through life, although a select few will realize they can face their inner fears and take control of the situation now. Some, however, will never face up and spend their lives being slaves to their own habits — never having taken the time to conquer their inner demons.

It's best to do it while you are young, and the monster is easier to tame. If you wait until you're older, it will be much more set in its ways and harder to conquer. Although it is still possible to master it at old age, I would recommend making your life easier and dealing with yourself now.

Luckily, I intend to help you by explaining various complex topics faced in adulthood and breaking them down for you in a practical manner that you can use not only to shape your life, but to determine where you want your life to go. Throughout this book, you will find I take you through brief exercises that will help you figure out what kind of life you want, and what steps you should take to get there.

The ability to take a conscious effort in making smart decisions, looking forward, and managing yourself is a vital first step in becoming an adult. Changing habits is only hard in the beginning, when you're constantly fighting against your own mind — but once it accepts things aren't so bad, you'll find yourself doing all sorts of amazing things as second nature. That is what it means to develop and grow as a human being, and developing your growth is a vital necessity in living a life that you can be proud of and enjoy.

Once you begin to take ownership of your life and do what you feel you enjoy, you have reached a point where you can contribute something to the world.

This is where many people make a mistake. Contributing something to the world does not mean doing amazing things like inventing the cure for cancer or becoming the next Elon Musk. Nor does it mean being an amazing person like a scientist, doctor, president, etc. Contributing to the world means finding a way to earn a living for yourself in such a way that it also adds some value to those around you. Do you think a bus driver contributes to the world? What about a janitor or a waiter?

The answer is obviously yes, and if you feel in your heart that can't be true, then I'd recommend thanking the bus driver next time he drops you off, or the janitor if you see him cleaning your school. The fact is, without people like this society simply wouldn't function the same. Remember during COVID-19 when "essential workers" were needed? Who were those essential workers? They were the people working in the checkout at your local Walmart.

So does that mean that you should go become a bus driver?

That depends on your current life circumstances, as well as your personality and temperament.

Most people become bus drivers because they have to, but there are a rare few who honestly simply enjoy driving around town and helping people get where they need to go. You can always spot the difference in the bus driver's eyes.

Your goal, therefore, is to prevent becoming a bus driver because you *have* to. Rather, you want to become what you *want* to be.

For some this comes easy, because life is handed to them. They will come from wealthy families, go to good schools, lead a comfy life filled with opportunities to succeed, and often if they "want" something, someone will "make" it happen for them. This does not mean their lives are easy. Sometimes wealthy people have dysfunctional and non-supportive families who break them down often. Also, our tendency to be jealous of them leads to them being treated with less compassion in certain settings.

That being said, most of us *want* to become something, and I can assure you that it won't be handed to you. To that end, we need to start asking ourselves hard questions about what we want, how we will go about getting it, and how we need to grow to reach that point. Once we have these questions, we need to think outside of the box and look at ourselves and our solutions in different ways so that we can get clever answers that won't boil down to "Well, I need to buy this thing I can't afford first," or, "I need to study at these places first and get these degrees, but I don't have the funds, so I guess it won't happen."

The most functional members of society get things done with no resources to start with. They think outside the box and find solutions to problems that others don't notice. More importantly, they look inside themselves and seek to see truths in their behavior and reasoning that they haven't noticed before. Doing all of this requires a skill that we can develop with some effort: lateral thinking.

***

Lateral thinking represents the first skill I want you to master. But what is it? You can argue that it simply is the ability to "think outside the box," yet there's a bit more to it than that. You see, lateral thinking is a concept first coined in 1967 by Edward de Bono, who actually wrote a whole book on the concept called *The Use of Lateral Thinking*. Here, he explains that people tend to think in a "step-by-step" manner that often delivers basic results. He argues that if we take a step to the side and create a new way of thinking, we arrive at unique solutions to problems, as well as unique answers to questions.

For the most part, how I interpret the concept is by understanding that it returns to our tendency to use a "pattern." Whenever we are faced with a problem, question, challenge, or new concept, we seek to frame it in a manner that we can compare it to what we have encountered before, and by making a comparison we hope to arrive at an answer with little effort. In other words, normal, traditional thinking leads to normal answers.

Yet there is a degree more nuance to this...

We all have an intrinsic uniqueness to us that stems from childhood. After that, we begin to mimic other kids on the playground before inevitably blending our uniqueness with whatever qualities our friends, parents, and societies instill into us. We effectively become painted snowflakes. Each of us is unique, yet with time we decide to paint ourselves blue for the sake of fitting in with the other blues, or purple so that we can have fun with all the other purple snowflakes.

Can I tell you a secret?

This is a good thing. It's normal and healthy.

Wanting to fit in with a group of people, wanting to fit into a community, is human. All human beings desire to become accepted members of their communities, and denying them this right is likely the cause of all the pain in the world. So I say we embrace this need to fit in, yet as we do so, we must understand that we will always be different.

So that is where we should begin to use lateral thinking: a special way of thinking, derived from our inner core of naturally thinking differently than others, to arrive at special answers that suit our reality more honestly and reflect ourselves a bit better.

Lateral thinking is commonly called horizontal thinking, whereas normal thinking is sometimes called vertical thinking. This description works well, as it describes the thought process in a way: with vertical thinking we start at the top (the input, aka the question/problem), then the thought simply moves from top to bottom in a straight line through us — in a step-by-step manner — before arriving at the answer (the output). This is the way to think that we are taught in schools, and it often works well for the sake of mass training a society on how to do complex things like math, physics, biology, etc. Traditional — vertical — thinking has a place in the world, but it isn't the only way to think.

Think back to when you first were taught to write. You were probably given a booklet that lets you practice step-by-step the whole process of producing an "A" over and over again. Here, vertical thinking shines, because the world would be chaos if each of us had an "out of the box" way of producing an "A." I simply say this so you don't start thinking that you were "taught wrong," or develop a superiority complex where you tell your friends they should "think more laterally."

We must remember there is a time and place for the different thought methods.

Now, we can finally start talking about lateral thinking (aka horizontal thinking). Here, we see that instead of starting at the top and going to the bottom (vertically), we instead take a step to the left, challenge our initial conclusions, and perhaps walk down to the bottom first before walking in reverse all the way back to the initial question.

In essence, we take our time to re-evaluate all our preconceived ideas and seek to incorporate new ideas from "outside" (horizontally). This is a fantastic method for generating new and often insightful ideas that not only sometimes best represent your desired way of doing things, but may (or may not) yield a massive improvement on a common solution to problems.

If you wish to improve your lateral thinking, I recommend the book *Lateral Thinking Lessons and Puzzles to Unlock Creativity and Leadership Ability.*

Let's look at some examples:

Let's say I'm Jeff, and two of my buddies and I recently went on a camping trip. When we arrived we realized we didn't bring a kettle, and thus couldn't make coffee.

The idea of camping without making coffee on the fire each morning was a disaster. Luckily, one of us had an obligation at the nearby church in town, so he would need to wake up at 5 a.m. and go into town the next morning.

If we think "traditionally" about the problem, then the solution becomes obvious. The guy going into town the next day should bring back a kettle. This is a solution that will give us a kettle to use for the next few days.

Easy, right?

Well…you see, the issue is that having an "obligation" at a church is much different than simply "attending" a church. He had responsibilities beyond the ceremony, both social and technical, that he had to deal with before bringing us a kettle to place on the fire.

So there the other guy and I sat, in the early morning beside a fire. We were woken up at 5 due to our friend failing to leave "quietly," and found ourselves up quite early in the morning, having eaten a can of baked beans for breakfast. Sadly, no coffee was had along with it.

6 a.m. arrives, yet alas, no coffee. 7 a.m. comes, and still no coffee in sight.

We began to realize we might well wait until 10 or 11 before the kettle ever even touches a fire. As desperation began to set in, we began looking to make a plan.

This is where lateral thinking starts to kick in. Now, we take a step to the side and look at the problem from various angles.

We need to heat some water. Do we need a kettle for that? It feels like the answer "should" be a yes, but honestly, no... we don't *need* a kettle to boil water. We had to challenge our preconceived notions on how to boil water. Can we make another plan? Which methods of heating water exist beyond the fire? Could we use the sun? Sure, if we could magnify it. Is there electricity available somewhere? The car battery! Do we know how to leverage these forces? Do we have the needed materials and tools? No, we don't.

Thus we go deeper and challenge our pre-trained notions further.

What is a kettle? What property does it have that makes it so needed?

The answer: metal.

A kettle is made of metal, and any metal will do.

Let's look further outside the box. Which metals can be used to contain water and placed on a fire?

Do we have metal bowls? No.

A pan? No.

Tinfoil? No.

Eventually, we came to realize that the old can of empty baked beans we had for breakfast represented the only way for us to make coffee. We found something we could use to filter it, and began to wash out the can before placing it on the fire.

Voilà!

When our friend arrived with a kettle, we were already sitting there with coffee in hand. We had additionally already discussed the feasibility of making scrambled eggs in a beer can, and explained to our friend that we could solve all our cooking needs by finishing all the beer first. Luckily, our friend also brought a pan along with the kettle.

There are also many references to lateral thinking in TV and pop culture.

In the hit TV show *Breaking Bad*, we see the anti-hero and protagonist Walter White (a school teacher forced into cooking meth to pay for his fight against cancer) finding himself stuck in the middle of the desert with an RV full of meth. Sadly, the battery to the RV is dead and it won't start. His options seem limited. He can't abandon the vehicle or else he may perish in the desert. He can't wait for help either, or else they will find him there — with the meth. The fact is that all his options seem to result in either jail or death — at least, if you think vertically, and conclude his only options are abandoning the vehicle or waiting for help.

Yet, thinking horizontally, Walter understands that the central issue is the lack of electric charge in the battery. If he could generate enough energy to produce a single spark and ignite the engine, he is saved. The solution? He uses his understanding of chemistry, as well as the meth lab he had in the back of the RV, to make a makeshift battery. Ultimately, he saves himself by thinking outside the box.

Interviewers also like to occasionally ask lateral thinking questions to potential employees in order to gauge their ability to use this form of thought. I personally think this approach is misguided, as often only "one" answer is correct, yet in truth laterally thinking often yields many viable answers. A true lateral thinker can envision multiple solutions to a problem, the answers only being correct when they are feasible. I, therefore, submit these for you to read, yet I need you to understand each *feasible* solution that still falls in line with the requirements is viable (even if your job interviewer insists there is only one correct answer).

For example:

A man is found dead hanging in a barn. He hung himself with a rope that is 10 feet long, and he is hanging 3 feet off of the floor. The room is completely empty, and the nearest walls are 20 feet away. It is clear that it was impossible to climb the walls or rafters, so how did he hang himself?

The classic answer to the question is that he stood on a 3-foot-tall block of ice which melted when he hung himself. For me, I find this answer quite fanciful (who has a 3-foot-tall block of ice?). However, many websites will argue it is "ingenious" since it requires you to account for the changing states of matter.

I found two others of my own: The first and most obvious is that someone helped him (an assisted suicide or murder), the second being that he stood on the back of a barn animal, such as a horse or cow, which left the room when he hung himself.

There are others, of course.

Which ancient invention that is used to this day is used to look through a wall?

Windows.

Technically, a "doorway" or "archway" works as well. You could also argue a well-positioned mirror can achieve the same result, albeit such an approach is not "commonly" used for looking outside; so it somewhat isn't viable given the constraints of the question.

The importance here is that your common notion of what it means to "look through a wall" is questioned.

When you normally hear such a sentence, you begin to think of Superman's X-ray vision, or at least a video camera. Yet the question never implied that the wall needs to be untouched. A broken wall is still a wall after all. So what does it matter if you cut a hole in it?

In that sense, even your assumptions of what a wall is must be questioned.

There are many, and I do love exploring them; however, next I will list my last one.

A man falls out of the window of a 30-story building, yet lands safely on his feet. Unaided by luck, any special equipment, or a specialized landing area—without the assistance of anyone—he is uninjured and immediately walks away. How did he do it?

The answer to this lies in the fact that we never specified the floor he fell out of. Nor do we constrain "how" he falls. The answer? He jumped out of a ground floor window. I personally argue that you could also say he jumped onto a nearby balcony or the roof of an adjacent building, since the question never specifies how "far" he falls.

I find that the irony of interviewers asking these lateral thinking questions is that they fail to intrinsically grasp what lateral thinking is when they expect a singular correct answer.

The truth is all answers that "solve" the problem in a logical way require lateral thinking. Notice, however, that some are better than others. It makes far more sense for a man in a barn to use the assistance of an animal to hang himself than to argue he somehow has access to 3-foot tall blocks of ice. It also makes far more sense that a man would willingly jump out of the window on a ground floor than to argue he would jump onto the roof of a building next door.

Also, I want you to notice that just because a solution requires lateral thinking does not mean it *is* lateral thinking. Lateral thinking will enable you to find various solutions to problems, yet coming up with multiple solutions does not mean you actually used lateral thinking. You may have made lucky associations or perhaps have seen various methods of solving problems in the past.

No, lateral thinking is the ability to challenge what you assume to be true, identify the "core" of a problem, and then move beyond the constraints of your traditional thinking to seek alternate paths to deal with the "core" issue. It requires a willingness to assume there are other options beyond what you can see, and that things can be changed if we are willing to accept they can be used beyond their original purpose. For example, ice can melt, animals can move, beer cans can be re-fashioned into cooking tools, etc. Then, we also need to look at the problem again and again, constantly challenging our current perspective on the matter and forcing ourselves to view them in new lights. In this way, we can often find many solutions to problems.

To illustrate, what happens when I say the word yellow? What does "yellow" make you think about? Chances are good it was a banana, or the sun, or perhaps a flower. In niche cases, you were likely thinking of something personal to you like the color of a yellow shirt, your yellow car, or the yellow walls of your house.

But what about trees? Can they be yellow or are they green?

Take a moment to reflect on this.

Chances are good you said a tree can be yellow, given that it is autumn, and the leaves are turning brown.

That would be true, but for many people the answer was reached vertically, as they remembered the leaves do turn yellow during autumn.

But what if I'm talking about spring, where the leaves are green? Can the green leaves still be yellow?

Take a moment to reflect on this. Can you find a way for green leaves to be yellow?

The answer, of course, is that they can undoubtedly be yellow, given that the sun is setting, and a yellow hue is painted over the green leaves, making them appear yellow as you look at them from the right angle.

I didn't take you through all this for the sake of making you feel inferior for your lateral thinking ability, nor that my lateral thinking abilities are superior (in fact, I was cheating; I can see a yellow tree outside my window right now. Normally it would be green, but the sun has cast various shades of gold and honey across the normal deep green I would expect).

The purpose of this whole investigation of color was to make you aware of your own assumptions and how they define your thinking. You assume yellow is a color for a banana or a flower, whilst green leaves can in turn *not* be yellow. Yet simply by forcing our minds to accept that those preconceived notions are wrong and tasking it to seek how it is possible for green leaves to be yellow, with time your brain will eventually give you solutions. The more you can force it to look beyond the first solution, the further you gaze across the horizon into the distance, searching for something that is there, even though you cannot see it—making mental leaps from the changes of autumn to the changes of light as the sun sets—you will eventually find a solution to a problem.

In the end, the point is this. First assume something is possible, then continuously investigate it without "settling" for an easy answer that doesn't feel good enough.

You need to do this, especially when applying lateral thinking to yourself.

*\*\**

Up till now I only ever discussed the idea of lateral thinking on outside scenarios and objects. But what about your heart and your dreams?

Let's say you want to become a doctor. Why?

Is it about money? Do you want people to treat you a certain way? Do you want to prove something to someone else?

You may have many preconceived notions at play in answering these questions. If you want money, why be a doctor? There are other ways to make money in this world.

If you want to be treated with high regard, perhaps you should rather find the people who treat you that way regardless of your status. Perhaps try to learn to let go of the idea of getting someone else's approval. Why are you assuming you need approval from others? Did it ever occur to you that you could simply give it to yourself?

Perhaps you feel your poor grades somehow prove something is wrong with you, and you won't succeed.

Did it occur to you that simply isn't true? In my own life, I was a student who got straight C's and never much for studying, up until the point an executive vice president of a large company took a liking to me and offered to be a mentor. That one act of someone believing I had massive potential and could succeed resulted in me having qualified for the National Honors Society in senior year with a slew of scholarships.

The thing is, just because your grades are poor now doesn't mean they always will be. You just need to find one reason to convince yourself you are capable, and challenge the idea that you aren't good enough.

Applying lateral thinking to yourself means assuming you can do things without proof, in a way that is honest and realistic, and allows for the idea that your life could look wildly different than you imagine in 3 years' time.

The truth is you have no clue what the future holds, nor does anyone else. Never place unneeded limitations or expectations on yourself. Always try to view the various potential angles of your life, and consider that there are sides to you that you don't even know yet.

In the words of Socrates: "The only true wisdom is in knowing you know nothing."

Of course, that also applies to the world around you. The world is simply filled with people who are doing what was always done before.

Take the story of Netflix, for example. Did you know it originally started as a traditional DVD rental store back in 1997? Here, the CEOs sought to think laterally and asked themselves why DVDs needed to be rented from a store in the first place? Wouldn't it be great if you could simply rent the DVDs online and have them delivered to your door in the mail like an amazon package? What if people could buy a subscription and have as many DVDs delivered to them as they pleased for that month?

Obviously, there were many holes in the ideas, but it still had the embers of success. The CEOs simply continued to assume they were onto something and continued challenging norms and assumptions. Wouldn't YouTube be great if you could watch movies on there? Perhaps our online DVD store could do that?

The rest becomes history. Simply because both DVD stores and YouTube existed, doesn't mean that they are doing it "right." Lateral thinking in a way that challenges yourself, society, and the way you think often leads to improvements of ideas.

This will be a great challenge you face. You will need to understand that the world isn't perfect, nor are you. After I got into CAU with my scholarships I made the mistake of thinking it would be smooth sailing and took the scenic route, this resulted in me losing the scholarships and having to take on some student debt.

That's the thing about adulthood. You'll never reach a point where everything is just "sorted." You have to accept that there will be ups and downs; sometimes you will be weak, other times you will be strong. You just need to never lose focus on one thing:

Always adapt.

People misquote Charles Darwin when he said "survival of the fittest"; if you go and read his work, what you will find is that he was talking about how only those who can *adapt* will survive.

***

Now let's talk about the world around you for a bit. Currently, it's filled with people who have answers. It's full of people who know what THE TRUTH is, and what you need to do to get it. Many people will come to you and say "You need to do X, Y, and Z to be a good person" or "This one simple rule guides my life" or "There are two kinds of people. red and blue", the worst of all: "If you can't do X, you will never do Y." As a rule, each of them is lying. I can assure you that each and every person who comes to you with an "answer" for the world is lying. You can always listen to what they have to say if they seem to have a point, but always only believe 60% of it and assume their opinions will change in 5 years.

After college I found myself working 20 odd jobs, starting various careers, getting married, having a child, and getting divorced. Then, after 16+ years in the navy where I found some good footing and developed a code with which I live a good life. As a rule of this code, I can assure you there are no absolute truths.

I started out with all this thinking I was going to become famous as a hip-hop artist.

Since then it was a journey of continuous change and various lessons before I could arrive at this point where I feel I have something I can offer you. It's not a whole truth, it's just something about the nature of life that has affected me as well as everyone I've met.

Life is about change. You might be successful and handsome now, but that won't necessarily be the case in 3 years. You may feel lonely, and unlovable now, but perhaps in 3 years that will be wildly different. I do not offer you this truth as absolute truth, but I do offer it to you as the only wisdom I see that applies to my life as well as the lives of others, and I must say it's a good thing. It means we can guide our own path if we are willing to be patient.

For you, this means asking yourself questions about what it is you desire for your own life. Ask yourself if the community you live in will agree, and then accept you won't fit in and will need to do it your own way anyway.

Once you do this you can begin managing your behavior and your patterns. You can align them with your goals and go forth seeking them. In order to do this, you must learn to accept yourself. This will require that you take some time to reflect on your flaws and shortcomings and realize they are a part of you, once you've accepted them you can change them, but only after accepting them.

Each of us, tragically, is a puzzle piece that won't fit into most puzzles. That's okay. In an ironic way, the fact we are each so different ultimately unites us. You are inherently free to do whatever you want simply because it's what everyone else is doing. In this world, there are no experts, professionals, or masters. There are only those who understand change is good.

Change requires patience. Change allows us to grow when we take a hand in guiding it, and when we grow of our own choice, we begin to become functional adults.

Before you can even take that step, you must begin to ask yourself the right questions and learn to accept who you are.

# WHAT IS ADULTING?

U nderstanding what it means to be an adult means understanding what it means to be human (Yes, we will now be touching on a high topic.) Tragically, however, the act of trying to define a human leaves us in a position where we have little else to compare ourselves to.

In order to reach any strong conclusions when investigating a topic, it is often best to draw comparisons between other "similar" examples. In our case, we need to draw comparisons with other "sentient" lifeforms that perform a variety of complex things for seemingly no immediately obvious reason (art, culture, music, recreational sex, politics, science, and philosophy).

Sadly, there seem to be no aliens around for us to study, nor have the heavens yet contacted us for a debate on good vs. evil (at least not since the Bible).

So that leaves the pickings very slim in terms of making comparisons, it leaves us with only one choice: animals.

Making comparisons between ourselves and animals may seem wise, we both share flesh and blood, we both feel pain and joy, and we undoubtedly share similar evolutionary goals — indeed, we even share DNA and ancestry. However, we must remain cognizant that the similarities starkly end there. You see, one cannot compare the claws of a lion to the claws of a Labrador, nor can one compare the wings of an eagle to the wings of a chicken. So how could we compare the minds and behavior of humans to those of any other animals?

Our minds *are*, after all, our most defining feature. It represents our evolutionary superpower. Much like how a lion's claws are vital to its deadliness, and a hawk's wings are paramount to its aerial dominance, so too are our brains what makes human beings elevate themselves beyond our baser animal origin to a point where we instinctively liken ourselves to something higher. All cultures and religions on earth acknowledge first and foremost that humans are beyond other animals, the Bible opens by saying we are made in God's image, so, too, does Shakespeare draw attention to this when his character Hamlet laudably exclaims:

"What a piece of work is a man! How noble in reason! How infinite in faculty! ... In action how like an angel! In apprehension how like a god! ... The paragon of animals!"

It is for this reason any and all comparisons to animals, especially regarding behavior as complex as adulthood and societal contribution, becomes an exercise of making hopeful observations, drawing rough conclusions, then taking a bit of salt when internalizing those conclusions. We *need* to look at ourselves as animals for the sake of having an example of "normal" behavior, sure, but only to a point. You see, one of the hardest things about trying to learn about being an adult is finding a good example. Even when we have them, conveying their experience becomes hard, because the truth is their childhood and lives are so riddled with complexity that the core truth can be hard to obtain — especially when we view them from the outside.

This leaves us in a precarious situation where we will need to begin investigating the core essence of what it means to be human by making evolutionary conclusions, revolving around animals, knowing that all of them must be taken with a grain of salt...

***

The first and most obvious aspect we can draw our attention to is tool making, however here we see that many animals use tools. Crows, primates, and even crabs all make use of various tools in various situations. Crows will frequently manipulate objects in order to obtain food, and apes not only use sticks to harvest insects from small places, but they will also sharpen sticks into spears for hunting bush babies. In crabs, we find that they will make use of shells for camouflage and protection, and the boxer crab is known to use stinging anemone as a protective weapon against predators.

Because of the fact that tool making exists in various different animal kingdoms (birds vs. primates vs. crustacean, as well as many others), we find ourselves forced to conclude that toolmaking is nothing special, in fact, it seems to have evolved independently several times in nature; creating the argument that any life containing world may indeed play host to tool using creatures. There is however one observation we can make…

In all the above animal examples, tools are only ever made with a degree of "immediacy" in mind. Often in these animals, we find that sticks, shells, or anemones are only ever "used" when the purpose is immediately apparent and beneficial to the animal. In humans however this is not nearly the case, when we make spears, we do it with long-term foresight, often making it several months in advance of its use (with a whole war or hunting trip anticipated as well). Even more so, we build the spear *to last*. We anticipate the fact it will break, and fashion it from metal. We consider what others may think when seeing it; and adorn it with sigils, symbols, words, and various colors to give onto our spear the ability to invoke admiration or fear in the minds of others, or perhaps even bravery in our own minds when we are scared.

Thus, we can from the "use of tools" infer our earliest observations on human nature: we think ahead. Within this vision of the future, we will focus on a variety of things, ranging from relationships, emotions, resources, our own emotions, living conditions, dreams, fears, etc. This trait of foresight is obvious in all functional adults, and in those who we see a shortcoming we often find that although foresight is had, it is often deflected, avoided, ignored, or even sparks fear and can lead to needless panic and a lack of positive thinking. Yet those who can wield foresight with a degree of "certainty" that they can solve their problems, while also acting upon them, will often find themselves becoming adults one way or another.

The next trait we should ponder is our ability to cooperate, a property of human nature cemented in fact. Let us not be fooled by fictional works such as *Game of Thrones*, *The Purge*, or *Lord of the Flies*, which claim that humans are inherently evil, cruel, and savage when left to our own devices. The truth is we tend to latch onto these stories because they invoke within us our deepest fears that we may be alone, and they entrance us with the dangerous prospect that we should fear our neighbors; as animals ourselves, this recognition of danger is strong enough to triumph the truth. The truth, however, is that a situation like what is described in the book *Lord of the Flies* had already taken place in real life.

Indeed, for those who don't know, the book *Lord of the Flies*, which tells a tale of children turning savage after a plane crashes on an island is a work of pure fiction, a fiction that was devised by a man who was later discovered to be a very cruel school teacher who liked bullying his students, pitting them against each other, and had a very stark outlook on life leading him to bouts of depression and alcoholism throughout his life. Although his work was lauded as a "breakthrough" observation of human nature, this was only done because of our human tendency to "feel" tragedy and fear. Later, various investigations and uncovering revealed the conclusions reached in *Lord of the Flies* were quite fanciful indeed.

This uncovering was done by a Danish historian, Rutger Bregman, who did a lot of investigations into mankind's obsession with its own darkness. He concluded our obsession with our dark insides was unfounded and chronicled much of his research and efforts in his book *Humankind: A Hopeful History*; what's more, he interviewed an Australian captain who had indeed rescued a group of Australian boys stranded on an island for over a year, much like *Lord of the Flies*, on the island of Tonga. What did he uncover? Not only did the school children not regress into a group of savages, but they actually worked together and built shelters, a gym, a water collection station, rationed food, and got along quite happily. When one of them fell off a cliff and broke a leg, the others carried him all the way back to camp and built a makeshift nursing room for him. The teenagers splinted his leg, cared for him, fed him, and when the time for rescue came, the leg was perfectly healed.

The historian was also able to research and chronicle explanations for complex events like genocide and war that still aligned with his belief in "human kindness," in WW2 he uncovered that most German soldiers *weren't* fighting for Hitler at all, rather, they were fighting to keep each other alive against the American and Russian onslaught. Likewise, another fact not commonly known to many, is that most soldiers of the apartheid government weren't fighting within the Angolan borders for the sake of oppressing the ANC or any given race, they were fighting against communism. At the time Mandela's underground party, the ANC, was aligned with the USSR. Although the Apartheid government's global goal was oppression, the people serving under them were more focused on combating communism than serving any tenets of racial cruelty.

The only reason any of this is worth mentioning is because when we investigate mankind's tendency to cause mass suffering, we often see it is seldom for the sake of committing acts of evil or the dogma of some dark ideologies. Although that may occasionally be the case for some, for most, we find people often align with the wrong side in a misguided quest to stand on the side of "good," and are often in search of a sense of belonging.

You see, when we attempt to view humans as animals, we find that we are pack animals. Not like wolves nor like herds of cattle, we don't necessarily have hierarchies like primates or lobsters (contrary to Jordan Petterson's beliefs on the matter), we form communities, we always seek to expand and grow those communities; and when we encounter a different community, that is when the fighting starts. Not for the sake of annihilation, but rather for the sake of protecting our own people; the people we care for.

This is where we can begin to move away from explaining and comparing our animal sides and moving onto the quintessential core of what it means to be human, and by extension, what it means to be an adult.

You see, human beings across the globe, independent of each other, always strive to establish societies wherein various individuals would seek to perform various roles in order to serve the greater community. Studies have found that "simple" environments tend to force our personalities to differentiate (Montiglio et al., 2013), meaning that in a simple "tribe" setting, our personalities diversify most probably toward the goal of meeting various needs within the group (fighter, mediator, commentator, leader, caretaker, etc.). More interestingly, these studies also highlighted that socially "complex" environments seem to lower the intensity of these personality differences because they became more adaptive.

It would be easy to interpret this to mean that as we move through various environments and friend groups (school, college, work, different friend groups); we tend to bend our personalities more to serve a role within the group, and with practice, we become better at controlling the various natural tendencies of our personalities.

It is remarkable how our hearts strive to serve each other. It seems to be a universal trait of people, so much so that we'll either adapt ourselves to accommodate whoever we're stuck with or change to fit in somewhere.

This is a plight I have deep sympathy for… In my mid-20s I found myself working hard, always stressed, fearful, and alone. A deep weight came to rest on my shoulders regarding what my future may look like, and if it would always be like this. I was doing everything right, I was working a 9 to 5, doing chores, trying to see my friends on the weekends, and generally trying to "adult."

However, as I was doing this I always felt so stressed and uncertain…I couldn't escape the feeling that it can't go on like this. I looked around me and noticed everyone else also looked stressed, and when I turned to many people who seemed to "have it together" for answers, I would be met with an expression that would echo the sentiment, "Hey… you should have learned this long ago. Why haven't you?"

This feeling of doing something wrong can be a painful mark, but I want to relieve you with the knowledge that we will carve a way out of it.

For the most part, much of this feeling lies in how hard it can be to find our purpose. No matter what, we want to live a meaningful life, yet we often find ourselves barraged with various opinions about what this looks like. We tend to fool ourselves that a meaningful life may have something to do with success, achievement, or money; but that is just the lie of television.

Being raised by TV, YouTube, and social media, many grow up thinking they must do something "amazing" or "outstanding" to be of value to the world.

In truth, much of what brings meaning will be different and unique for each of us. More importantly, much of what brings us meaning is not found in our major achievements, but rather in living a life in which we can feel ourselves giving back. As individuals, our social wiring drives us to seek what makes us "special", and on this road, we will often climb many obstacles and claw at dreams in the hope that they will fulfill us.

Tragically, since much of this effort is fueled by the "fantasy" of what we think will fulfill us, rather than the reality, we often find ourselves broken on this onward march toward living a meaningful life.

Yet this is the opposite of our nature. We seek what makes us special not for what will make us "special" in the sense that we will be valuable, but rather for what will make us uniquely useful to our community and families. Perhaps even society in a broad sense. This does not require us to do amazing things, it requires us to care for others and provide for them.

This dynamic finds its roots in the nature and purpose of our childhood, you see, human children take *very* long to grow up fully. A deer is born and is immediately able to start running and thinking. A lion cub, after a few brief weeks of needing care, enters a stage where it already seeks to play and "pretend" fight with its siblings, ultimately being a full-grown lion in less than 3 years.

With humans this is an entirely different matter, in our case, it would be wiser to compare our development cycle to that of a kangaroo, where the baby joey is born prematurely, no larger than a small insect, and will spend the next several months suckling and growing within its mother's pouch. Although we are not born as insects, we are born wholly helpless with underdeveloped brains, immune systems, and even skeletons and muscles. Scientists estimate that we are born approximately 12 months prematurely when compared to other primates, meaning pregnancy should technically have lasted up to 21 months in order for us to be as well developed as other primates at birth.

In our case, much of this is due to the astronomical amount of energy and fuel that goes into feeding our brain, which can consume several times more energy than any other part of our body, since our brains are actually densely packaged with a far higher amount of neurons than what is found in other animals. Scientists initially believed the reason we are born so prematurely was due to the small birth canal available to us, however further research poked some minor holes in the theory and a partial shift is occurring toward the idea that we are born at 9 months because it would have been impossible for our mothers to eat enough food to sustain our brain development.

By giving birth early, that immense loss of energy is halted and instead the whole process is slowed. What might have taken months becomes stretched out over years, giving us the various stages of childhood we all have experienced at one time or another in our lives. During these childhoods, we are very reliant not only on our parents for food and shelter, but also on our community for engagement and a sense of discovery and emotional interaction. There is an African proverb that says:

"It takes a village to raise a child."

You see, childhood is about taking from the community. Adulthood is about giving back. Becoming a provider. Not just for your children but for your neighbors, friends, fellow hobbyists (Bakers, painters, cyclists, toy makers), or country. Whatever you associate with really. Whatever aspect of the world or group of people you feel drawn to, as long as you begin to give back to that community on some level, then you'll slowly become happier with yourself.

\*\*\*

Now, this is where adulthood comes in... You see, before you can even begin to consider giving back to the community, you first need to learn how to take care of yourself. You will have no ability to give a beggar a few dollars if you are a beggar yourself. Maslow's hierarchy of needs becomes a prime template for how to navigate this.

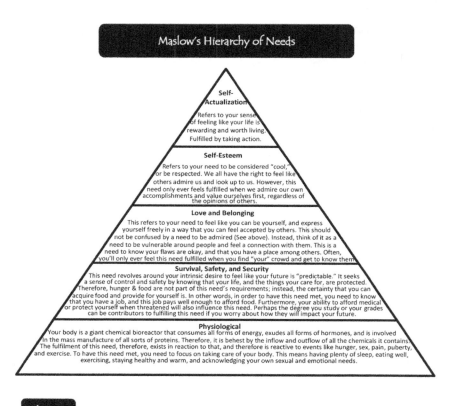

Maslow's Hierarchy of Needs

**Self-Actualization**
Refers to your sense of feeling like your life is rewarding and worth living. Fulfilled by taking action.

**Self-Esteem**
Refers to your need to be considered "cool," or be respected. We all have the right to feel like others admire us and look up to us. However, this need only ever feels fulfilled when we admire our own accomplishments and value ourselves first, regardless of the opinions of others.

**Love and Belonging**
This refers to your need to feel like you can be yourself, and express yourself freely in a way that you can feel accepted by others. This should not be confused by a need to be admired (See above). Instead, think of it as a need to be vulnerable around people and feel a connection with them. This is a need to know your flaws are okay, and that you have a place among others. Often, you'll only ever feel this need fulfilled when you find "your" crowd and get to know them.

**Survival, Safety, and Security**
This need revolves around your intrinsic desire to feel like your future is "predictable." It seeks a sense of control and safety by knowing that your life, and the things your care for, are protected. Therefore, hunger & food are not part of this need's requirements; instead, the certainty that you can acquire food and provide for yourself is. In other words, in order to have this need met, you need to know that you have a job, and this job pays well enough to afford food. Furthermore, your ability to afford medical or protect yourself when threatened will also influence this need. Perhaps the degree you study or your grades can be contributors to fulfilling this need if you worry about how they will impact your future.

**Physiological**
Your body is a giant chemical bioreactor that consumes all forms of energy, exudes all forms of hormones, and is involved in the mass manufacture of all sorts of proteins. Therefore, it is behest by the inflow and outflow of all the chemicals it contains. The fulfilment of this need, therefore, exists in reaction to that, and therefore is reactive to events like hunger, sex, pain, puberty, and exercise. To have this need met, you need to focus on taking care of your body. This means having plenty of sleep, eating well, exercising, staying healthy and warm, and acknowledging your own sexual and emotional needs.

**Theory:** When it comes to these needs, you need to understand that your body and mind will exist in a state of continuously interacting and shifting between them regardless of how well the needs at the bottom are met. In other words, even if you live a lonely, sexless, hunger-filled life of homelessness, despondency, and dire failure. It is still possible to feel moments of good self-esteem or a sense of self-actualization. The thing is, this will just happen more infrequently and will be hard to maintain and reach for, since you'll be more concerned over your survival and your hunger. Therefore, by meeting the lower needs well, we free ourselves to reach higher up the pyramid.

Here, we find that the needs a human must have satiated are represented. In the pyramid, needs placed near the bottom take a higher "priority" than those that are placed on top. This means that your instincts will gravitate to meet your physiological needs (food, water, shelter, sex, sleep) before it will endeavor to meet the need for safety (security, predictability, medical care, lack of fear, lack of danger, financial certainty).

A common misconception of the hierarchy is that higher needs cannot be met when lower ones are still lacking. This is untrue, as it is often the case that you will often find yourself weaving in between the various needs as you go about seeking to satiate yourself, usually moving on when a need is "somewhat" satisfied, even if only temporarily.

What is most intriguing, however, is that the four lower needs called: physiology, safety, love/belonging, and esteem are all described as "deficiency" needs, meaning our yearning to satiate them is done more for the sake of avoiding unpleasant feelings like hunger, fear, or loneliness, rather than for the sake of gaining something.

The final need, known as "self-actualization," represents a need that is wholly reflective of achieving a feeling of higher purpose. In other words, it is reflective of your need to be valuable to the community and for your life to have meaning. This need is the only "growth" need on the hierarchy as it focuses solely on trying to feel something it normally wouldn't, meaning it is pursued solely for the sake of feeling a sense of fulfillment.

Notice that, although you can work on satisfying your need to achieve "self-actualization" while hungry, your need for hunger will often attempt to overwhelm your need for self-actualization, which often leads to a frustrating scenario where you will pursue matters other than what will truly fulfill you. To counter this, the best solution is to try and gain mastery of your life in a way that gains control of the situation revolving around your lower needs. You need not satisfy them wholly, only enough that your focus can shift to other matters.

In fact, one of the more core acts of adulthood is the ability to momentarily suspend one of your needs for a few months (or even years) for the sake of satiating another more permanently. It is quite possible to ignore or preferably accept your loneliness (lack of love) as you seek to improve your security or esteem first. Likewise, you can attempt to self-actualize without living in a safe environment, or even being sure where your next meal comes from. The important part is to realize that your life is not simply going to be the act of meeting one of these needs; it will be the act of trying to meet all of them.

This hierarchy of needs will often represent the reason parents have children, children go to college, or even why people join the military (to go to college after).

As a first step, you should begin by writing down which needs you feel are lacking in your life and why (*Lacking*), then ask yourself what steps you need to take to satisfy these needs (*Next steps*). Next, you can also quickly write down what makes them feel satisfied, and why (*Met by,*) and reflect on a moment of gratitude for them (*Gratitude*). Throughout the book I'll provide some examples on how to do journaling exercises, one such example is below. Take a good 20 minutes thinking about this, as often things tend to pop up in hindsight that deserve to be written down, some may even feel interconnected, and you'll need to take some time to ponder where they fit in the hierarchy. Once you have written out your needs, what meets them, and what doesn't, in your own journal, for your final step I want you to go and ask yourself, *What should I be doing to meet my missing needs?*

Preferably, you should seek to start at the bottom, however, if you notice that an immediate (time-sensitive) opportunity is available to meet a higher one, consider which of the lower needs to momentarily suspend as you pursue it. I recommend you fill in the exercise on the next page based on the instructions I gave above.

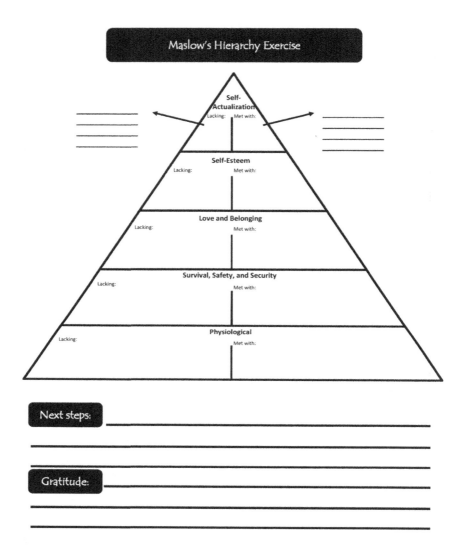

In a few months, come back to this list and ask yourself what has been satisfied. Take a moment to either congratulate yourself; or, if you failed, ask yourself what you should do differently next. If you can reach a point where all your focus is placed on "self-actualization," then you can start working on affecting the world.

# 3

# BUILDING YOUR ARCHETYPE

One of the greatest challenges of entering adulthood is coming to terms with who you are. This is a matter that all human beings are, in one way or another, intrinsically drawn to, as our lives are often cluttered with us trying various things, hobbies, pursuits, and pleasures in an attempt to understand what clicks for us and what doesn't, with the end goal often being to find our "place" in the world.

Alas, this quest is often fraught with a myriad of distractions and those who are wise often notice that even when we move beyond the distractions we will find ourselves walking in a spiral, doomed to repeat many of our patterns over and over again.

Very often, we will find ourselves "unhappy", and launch a quest to uncover what makes us happy. For most of us this will mean simply trying out a new hobby. For those of us who are a bit more desperate, we'll find ourselves impulsively buying an airplane ticket to Nepal in an attempt to "uncover" who we are — or perhaps you'll dye your hair blue and get a few piercings…

I'll give it to you straight. No number of piercings, blue hair, conversations with monks in south-east Asian countries, or hobbies will ever truly tell you who you are. This is a pitfall many will run into on their quest of "discovering" who they are, as the term "discovering" often implies to them that they need to do a variety of quests, dress in a way that expresses their inner world or defines them, or even travel to places and experience things that will "awaken" their true worth. The problem is that all of this often is done under the impression that uncovering who you are is a matter of finding it along the way of your life. That is a lie.

In truth, people who really have "discovered" themselves understand that it is not a matter of dying your hair purple and finding a group of people that understand why. Discovering yourself is not an event that happens to you. Discovering yourself actually means two things:

First, looking at your past story and finding a way that owns it. Second, looking at who you want to be and taking the steps to achieve it.

***

In that sense, finding yourself is more a matter of embracing both your past and deciding your future, and finding a way to be happy about it. Once this is done then you will actually get a chance to truly express who you are, truly discover what you are good at in a realistic way, and ultimately understand that you have room to grow and develop.

Indeed, the act of finding yourself is not a game of hide-and-seek, it is an act of creation.

That last part is key. People who live truly happy lives have come to terms with the fact that they can still improve. They are not under the illusion that they are perfect, nor are they under the illusion that they are worthless. Truly happy people have somehow looked at their past, seen that they have shortcomings and imperfections, and embraced them.

As mentioned, this is the key first element: Embracing your past. Many of us have stories of our past that often serve some need of our ego. We can come from decent households, yet still cling to the idea our parents were cruel to us. We can have loyal friends in school, yet still, tell ourselves we were unwanted and perhaps bullied. Members of the opposite sex may have shown interest in us, yet still, we can look in the mirror and say no one wants us.

This is where the ego plays its cruel cards. It will tell you that your parents never gave you what you needed emotionally so that you can play the victim and tell others why you may be excused for coming short. Your ego will demand that you should be admired by many, and you will find yourself seeking the friendship of those beyond your current circle. Your ego will demand you be seen with only the most beautiful boys/girls, and therefore prevent you from appreciating the honest advances of another person. These are the burdens of an ego when you look into your past, it will weave excuses and demands into your stories that often will make you feel like a victim, make you feel undesired and unloved, and make you feel your needs were unmet.

I do not say these things to invalidate your truths. Perhaps your parents were abusive. Perhaps you felt your friends weren't truly there for you or you deserved to be treated better. Perhaps you wanted to be approached by more desirable suitors. Sure, but do not let these truths rest on your heart in a way that smothers it. If your parents were abusive do not buy into the illusion that it means you are broken and that it's okay to give up. Do not believe in the lie that you are alone when you are not, nor that you are unloved when you are.

You see, the issue is that when we look at these past stories in a way that demands the world give something to us, we often prevent ourselves from owning our stories. You will always find yourself demanding your parents be better. Demanding new or better friends. Demanding better suitors or telling your lovers they should be better. Instead, try to make whatever peace with your parents as they are. Turn your attention to whoever has been willing to be your friend and be thankful. Be willing to explore the love someone offers you, as it is always precious.

Most importantly, don't look at your past and tell yourself "it should have been like this," "I wish it was like that," "I wish I was better here," "I wish this person would've," "I wish I was good enough," "If only this had happened," "If only I was treated like..." (You see what I mean? This can go on forever because it is easy to make demands of your past and wish for something better.)

What are you left with? Regret, shame, pain, low self-esteem, some depression, and perhaps even a victim mentality (or worse, a guilt complex). Looking at your past like this is easy, and a way for your mind to try and cope with some of your shortcomings, but it is often unrealistic and puts you in a position where it is hard to grow.

I want to tell you something important.

It's okay if your past was awful.

It's okay if you were bullied, it doesn't prove anything is wrong with you.

It's okay if you were abused, it doesn't mean the scars it left are permanent, you can grow beyond them.

It's okay if some people didn't want your advances; one day the right person(s) will.

In the end: no matter what your past was — no matter how awful — you need to find a way to realize it is okay. You need to learn how to look in the mirror and say:

"This happened to me. It sucks, but it is okay, it proves nothing bad about me."

"That's how it happened, I can live beyond it. So what's next?"

***

Reaching this point is easier said than done. Often, it can feel impossible for us to move beyond our past because we can't forgive someone or let go of an injustice done to us. Perhaps even we feel the world cheated us or we weren't given a fair chance. This is okay; you don't need to forgive anyone, nor do you need to "like" what happened to you, the important part is that you make peace with it—own it—and realize you can live beyond it. For most people, it will take a few months of soul searching to reach that point. For many, it will require some therapy or the support and advice of good friends and family. Ultimately…it's possible; no matter who you are or what happened to you—it just takes some effort. And most importantly: It will take time.

There is, of course, good reason for achieving this first aspect of discovering yourself. The thing is, when we are seeking to discover ourselves it is more an act of creation than an act of discovery. As touched on previously, you cannot reach a point where you feel complete without first coming to terms with your past.

Why?

Because when you seek to bury your past with victimhood, shortcomings, sorry stories, and failure. You are inherently allowing your ego to cast a web of lies over who you are. You are deceiving yourself into thinking you either have no value, or you may think you are some unrecognized genius/savant, perhaps that you're an admirable martyr, or even deserving of special treatment due to your hard life. All of these conclusions are self-serving lies. All are untrue, and you will walk a painful life if you invest in them.

Although the painful elements of your story are true, the conclusions you reach from them often are not. This makes the act of making peace with your past and improving yourself impossible… The truth is whenever people ask you to "tell your story", you'll often begin a dramatic rendition of the tragedy that is your life and why you should be taken care of, rather than finding value in your past and trying to build from it. Furthermore, in believing in these lies, you will often fail to realize that you have some honestly admirable traits that can be made use of. Even worse, you may fail to see which aspects of your persona truly require improvement.

This is the core reason why we need to recognize and move beyond our past in a sincere, caring, and honest way. We need to do it for the sake of coming to terms with our own shortcomings and talents. This will allow us to understand how we can improve.

This is by far your best way of also knowing you have embraced your past. Those who have embraced their past need not explain away their errors or find excuses for their actions. Often, they have made peace with the fact that they are imperfect and have made mistakes, and view their history in a way that is sympathetic and caring, not hateful or regretful. Most importantly, they understand what they did wrong, what they did right, why they should be admired, and why they shouldn't.

Once you look at the most painful parts of your story in this way, you can begin to make peace with your whole story. Because your story is more than just pain, there were happy moments and you have indeed also done a few things right.

You can and should be aware of this and seek value in this. Even the most abusive of relationships often have glimmers of a silver lining, and the most tragic moments have rays of light. Once you stop the tears from clouding your eyes you will be able to see them.

***

Now, being armed with the truth of who you are and where you come from, you can seek to improve.

But why should you improve? And toward what end?

Very often, when we make peace with the past we often find ourselves in a position where we don't mind being "average" with regard to certain skills. In fact, you may have embraced the fact you are not a good singer or that you are not good at academics.

This is healthy. There is no reason to worry about these things nor seek their improvement if it doesn't serve you.

Of course, the shadow of a threat looms near... You see, even if you learn to be okay with your shortcomings. A need to always grow and improve yourself exists regardless of if you think you need it. Anything that doesn't grow stagnates. This applies to you as well, if you do not grow and develop your talents—or overcome your vices—then you will find yourself coming up short when trying to build yourself and become a functioning adult.

Toward this end, we must find motivation and reason. All expenditures of energy and effort should serve your long-term goals. This is why the second part of uncovering yourself lies in understanding what you want from your future.

There are two things we can glean from understanding what we want from our future: the first is a source of motivation. The second, is an understanding of our own wants and dreams… This second bit is quite pivotal, because in attaining and reaching for them we often come to understand ourselves more deeply and define ourselves more clearly.

Navigating our desires for the future might not be as straightforward as you may assume. For the most part, it becomes quite easy to follow lines of thought that revolve around wishful thinking and unrealistic standards, counterintuitively, this can often run hand in hand with the self-assessment that you may not be able to achieve your dreams and that you might not be good enough to do the things you want to do. Often, the idea may linger in the back of your mind that you just "am not that sort of person" and won't be able to pursue a desire based on an incorrect self-assessment of who you are.

Much of this can be solved by taking the first step of making peace with your past as we've discussed. Then, the art of plotting out your future becomes easier as you know where you are coming from. I don't want to overcomplicate this too much by talking about the ego again. It becomes far simpler and streamlined simply to say that you need to be honest with yourself. By being honest and realistic with yourself you are immediately overcoming many of the burdens the ego can bring.

We can now begin to navigate an exercise that I developed that has helped me personally in finding myself, which from this point forward we will be more correctly naming the act of creating myself.

The act of creating yourself begins first with an understanding of what you want. Toward that end, we are going to do an exercise where you will be writing down 20 things that you want for your future in your own journal. Twenty things may sound like a lot, but it becomes rapidly easy when you start to ask yourself the right questions and answer them honestly.

What kind of house do I want? Do I want a house, or do I want to live a more mobile lifestyle? Do I have an apartment? How do I want to spend my free time? What is my lifestyle? What do I eat? What are my hobbies? What kind of friends do I want? Do I have a girlfriend/boyfriend? What is this lover like? What do I do in my free time? Where do I live? Do I have pets? Do I have kids? Which school do those kids attend? What values do I want to teach them? Which values do I want to pursue? Did I study any degrees? What job do I have?

You can also make the list highly materialistic:

I want a jet ski.

I want a pool.

I want a collection of fancy watches.

I want my house to have a dedicated gaming room.

You can also make the list very abstract:

I want to be highly disciplined.

I want to be honorable.

I want to help the poor.

I want to assist with charity.

I want to serve my country.

I want to master an instrument.

I want to know a second language.

In the end, no matter how materialistic or abstract your list is, it won't matter. What truly matters is that you feel the items on it are an honest reflection of what you want for your future, especially in the next 5 years. Place them in the list below:

Once you have your list of 20 items that your future must contain, we are going to start to have a moment of realism and accept that most of the items on your list will never be obtained. Toward this end, we will be dividing the list into three categories.

The first category will be the "non-negotiable". Here, we will be placing two or three things that simply must be a part of your life in order for you to feel happy. The items on this list should be somewhat realistic and attainable, yet most importantly, vital for you to feel your life is worth living. Ideally, these should not be material things, but rather ideal values like: "a clean home" or "a modest savings account." For the most part, these items will act as a compass for the next moves you must make, so take some time to choose them wisely. Ultimately, they must be obtainable, and you must have some plan in mind for obtaining all of them.

The second category is the "flexible" list. Here, we aim to place 10 items that can be described as items that in one way or another, you ultimately imagine as a part of your life, yet you wouldn't feel too incomplete without them. Here, we will be placing things that you would like to have, yet you should still be able to make peace with living without them. In a sense, you could put a few of your less realistic choices here, but when all is said and done the items on this list should still be seemingly obtainable.

The final category will be our "bonus items." Here, we will be placing the items that we feel would be nice, but ultimately know we can live without them. These are still things that you want, however, now you will go and acknowledge that they are merely nice things, and not things that you will pivot your personal happiness upon. In essence, these are the things you want, yet can surrender if you must. Place the remainder of your list here.

Here is an example template of what you should be doing in your journal:

## List Priorities:

**Non-negotiable:**
_____
_____
_____

**Flexible:**
_____
_____
_____
_____
_____
_____
_____
_____
_____

**Bonus Items:**
_____
_____
_____
_____
_____
_____
_____
_____
_____
_____
_____

There are a few rules that we will be applying to this list. First, our goal is to obtain all the items in the non-negotiable slot no matter what. Second, we will accept the fact that we will only seek to obtain 70% to 80% of the items on the flexible list. Lastly, we only need one or two items from the "bonus items" list before feeling satisfied with it.

Notice that with this approach, we are still going to attempt to obtain some of our bonus items, we are just being honest with how we will go about doing it and setting a boundary for what is enough.

Now, this is where things can become interesting. You see, from this point forward we are going to delve into the world of personal archetyping. An archetype is an "outline" for a character often used by writers when designing the personas of their characters. Interestingly, the concept of archetyping also exists in the field of psychology where famous analytical psychologists like Carl Jung argue that we all have four archetypes within us (The persona, the anima/animus, the shadow, and the self), and that these four archetypes combine and recombine in various situations that form 12 other archetypes: The innocent, the orphan, the warrior, the caregiver, the seeker, the lover, the destroyer, the creator, the ruler, the magician, the sage, and the jester. All of these archetypes are said to become a part of us as we move through various stages of life, however, it must be noted that all of these archetype theories have not been as widely accepted in the field of psychology, even though many psychologists argue they carry some weight.

Luckily, for us, the method of archetyping I wish to discuss has little to do with literary tools or uncertain psychological theories. The method of archetyping I wish to discuss was developed by me and borrows from the power of the two above approaches of archetyping to create a tool that we can use to define and build ourselves into somebody we would like to be.

You see, the two above approaches both share an invaluable characteristic that anyone who begins a journey of self-discovery will find indispensable. They ask us to choose who we are (or want to be) first, before we even have any of the characteristics of the character we desire. Often people set out on a quest of self-discovery under the illusion that they will realize who they are, when in fact it is more a matter of deciding and accepting some shortcomings.

In fact, within literary theory, it is often preferred to deviate a character from a chosen archetype for the sake of making them interesting. Often creating a "flawed" version of an archetype that often is a much more relatable and realistic representation of a persona. When we seek to apply this concept to our own lives, this approach becomes wise as we will often have deviations from our desired archetype that often serve to bolster us with a "uniqueness" and a challenge we can overcome or adapt to in our journey of internal mastery.

So how do we go about archetyping ourselves? Well…we begin by looking at the list we just made in our most recent exercise — looking at our "non-negotiables," our "flexibles," and our "bonuses" — and asking ourselves:

Which type of person has these things?

Which type of person wants these things?

Which traits do they have that will allow them to obtain these items and live this life?

Which sort of person is like this?

Who must I become?

Write your answers to these questions in your own journal as outlined here:

## Archetyping exercise

Which type of person has these things?

Which type of person wants these things?

Which traits do they have that will allow them to obtain these items and live this life?

Which sort of person is like this?

Who must I become?

The answer to the question of your self-discovery lies buried in these questions, and by answering them honestly and as fully as possible you are ultimately allowing yourself a chance to look into your heart and see who it is you truly want to become, as well as a glimpse of who you are.

*** 

Now I'll be upfront with you. If you reread this chapter in four or five years' time and repeat these exercises you will find that many of the items in your list have changed and many of the answers you wrote above have changed. This is because who you are as a person always exists in constant change.

The difference between an adult and someone who is still living a juvenile life lies in the ability to take command of this eternal process of change that will be your life. You can choose to be a sailor who is thrown about and ravaged in the storms that life throws at you, or a captain who knew the storms would come and already decided how/where he will sail to move past them toward better waters. The art of self-discovery is a matter of making a choice in deciding who you want to be and moving toward it.

Thus, we arrive at our next exercise.

Take the answers you wrote above into account and ask yourself: who do I want to be? Take some time to write out this future version of yourself and all the things they have and will do for fun.

Who is your future archetype?

Then, we can now ask ourselves the next question: Who am I now? What version of myself am I now and what traits do I not yet have for becoming who I want to be?

Finally, list three to five traits that you feel you need to develop or overcome in order to be who you want to be. Here is some space to write all this:

## Development exercise

Who do I want to be?
_____
_____
_____
_____
_____
_____
_____
_____
_____
_____
_____
_____

Who am I now?
_____
_____
_____
_____
_____
_____
_____
_____
_____
_____
_____

Three to five traits I must acquire or lose:
_____
_____
_____
_____
_____

Once you have your three or five traits. We need to set some goals for them. This part is important because people tend to make a mistake here that often ends up with them shooting themselves in the foot.

Allow me to explain with an example. Let's say that you realized you tend to lack discipline and that in order to achieve your future archetype, you should be more disciplined. When I ask you to set some goals for this you may make the mistake of saying something like "starting tomorrow, I'll be more disciplined and start working out more." This almost always ends in failure for one simple reason: The goal is too vague. The problem is that "discipline" is an abstract concept that cannot be measured easily. We need to set goals we can measure on a daily level and immediately evaluate with a win/lose for the day.

To be fair, it is wise to try to measure it indirectly with another activity like exercise, yet then you still need to be realistic with yourself. For example, if you are the sort of person who hates exercise, then using it as a measuring stick for your discipline becomes unwise as you will often break yourself down each time you fail to work out (or you may even incorrectly say you failed because you did 15 push-ups instead of 30.) Often, it is best to set realistic goals that are relevant to your own life, and also set up a system where you can make a rebound when you fail.

In this example of discipline, we can use the act of going to the gym as a measuring stick so long we are cognizant of the reality of which requirements need to be fulfilled to measure "discipline."

Although it is true you can look at somebody who exercises themselves to death and say, "That person is disciplined," it would be more accurate to say that that person "works hard." In truth, in this scenario discipline has nothing to do with how hard you work out, but only in the fact that you decided to work out in the first place. Perhaps the only requirement should be to "go" to the gym, and not stress too much about what we do when we get there. Doing this, again and again no matter what, will slowly build some self-discipline, especially when we take the time to congratulate ourselves each time we walk through the entrance of the gym, even before we begin to work out.

Given how abstract and broad the concept of discipline is, we can actually apply it in a myriad of ways. Perhaps you tend to slack off with your studies. An exercise of discipline here would involve a commitment to open a book once a day, each day, and start reading. The quantity of reading is irrelevant, all that matters is the attempt to read as well as the high five you give yourself when you open up the book. With time, reinforcing this behavior will shape some discipline within you.

That being said, I now need to have a moment of honesty with you. When we seek to develop complex traits like discipline, we will find that we need to maintain them for three to four weeks minimum before they work. That means that if you go to the gym for three days before giving up, it doesn't count. As a rule, the formation of new behaviors requires at least 21 days.

This is what makes all this hard. You could try to sharpen your discipline by trying to exercise daily and opening up your books each day, yet even if you do it each day for 2 weeks and stop, it won't count.

I'm not saying this to discourage you, I'm saying it to you for the sake of helping you realize that if you fail at the 17-day mark. Try again, because you barely had a taste of what it feels like to grow and develop the trait you desire. I'm also trying to convey one other thing:

I'm trying to give you a goal.

In the following exercise I will task you with setting goals, and no matter what you must try and pursue them for at least 21 days before deciding "how things are going". Only then can we actually begin to tell ourselves we are refining our skills and growing. The most interesting of all, I've found in my own life it can even take up to two years for a new trait to fully settle in as you seek to find ways of squeezing it into your own persona and lifestyle. Regardless, I can assure you each person reading this is capable of developing, growing, or altering any trait they have with a consistent effort.

Now let us talk about the exercise:

For each of the three or five traits that you listed in the previous exercise that you need to develop, find at least two ways in which you can measure or track it (Increase this number to four or five methods of measurement if the trait is something abstract like empathy, discipline, joyfulness, etc.). As mentioned, your methods of measurement should be something that you can easily track and measure, and not be some "abstract" form of measurement that relies on vaguely observing your own behavior in an inconsistent way. It should be an activity or an exercise of sorts that you can repeat and track easily. You are welcome to consult the internet further with regards to this. If your desired trait involves other people, like developing a sense of humor, try to make an exercise like: at least once a day I'll try to crack a joke, even if it is in the mirror. List and discuss your measurement methods as shown:

## How will you go about measuring yourself?

Measurement methods:

_____
_____
_____
_____
_____
_____
_____
_____
_____
_____
_____
_____

Can they be empirically tracked?

_____
_____
_____
_____
_____
_____
_____
_____
_____

How will I reward myself for meeting my goals?

_____
_____
_____
_____
_____

Now you know what you want, who you want to be, which traits you need to hone to become that person, as well as a few exercises you can do to measure yourself.

I need to warn you of another pitfall that people will encounter when trying to improve these traits: Negative self-talk. I was hinting at this in my earlier example with exercise. You see, any task becomes impossible when you aren't motivating yourself and giving even your smallest efforts acknowledgments. Always seek to forgive your failures and congratulate yourself for trying. High-five yourself as you walk into the gym. Tell yourself you were awesome for walking up to a stranger and striking up a conversation, even if it was excruciatingly awkward. If you don't do this you'll often give up quickly when trying to grow.

The first time I used this archetyping method it was a bit different from what I wrote above. You see, at the time I was looking for a good woman and made a list of 20 traits she must have for me to be happy with her, and organized them according to how I explained above. I divided this list into "non-negotiables", "flexible", and "bonus". I decided that I'd be happy if she only had 80% of the items listed under flexible, and two of the items listed under "bonus", then I looked at this list and asked myself: "Would such a woman date a man like me now?" After a moment of looking at myself honestly, I realized the answer was no. I then asked myself: "What sort of a man attracts such a woman", and what ensued was a 10-year journey into becoming the man my wife enjoys today.

You are welcome to adapt and change the method slightly to suit your own reality as well. The important part is that you realize you need to improve, and set a clear definition for what that improvement should be. You need to define your future archetype and strive to become that person. You can even set an archetype for your desired career, called a "career archetype" that seeks to define your ideal career, or even for things like the "ideal roommate" or an "ideal lifestyle". The process of archetyping is quite flexible and capable of being used to come to an understanding of the various aspects of your life.

# LET'S MAKE
# A PLAN

Where am I going with all this talk of adulting, what people are, and archetyping? Well… Ultimately, we are moving to a point where we want to be making a plan for our future. This is intrinsically the core part that defines a functional adult from a non-functioning one. When all is said and done, adults spend their time thinking about their future in a way that generates value and leads to scenarios where they are somehow enriched. If you don't have a car, make reasonable plans to get one. If you don't like your current job, find a way out. If you are worried about someone stealing your car, make plans around this also. If you don't like your friends or find your love life lacing, reach out to others and experiment with new interactions.

Of course, much of this can sound scary… Very often the main thing holding us back from trying new things and from reaching our true adult selves is a fear that we are not ready, or not good enough. This is of course normal, as many people feel a sense of fear at the idea of having to take on additional responsibilities and do things they are not used to. However, I must warn you that you actually have very little choice in the matter… You will be forced to take on more responsibility no matter what. If you resist this and try to run away you will more likely than anything find yourself a beggar in a few years' time, or perhaps stuck at your local McDonalds. This means that if you don't want to find yourself trapped at the bottom rung of society, you have two choices. Either be forced to reluctantly accept more responsibility as you grow up, or choose of your own volition to embrace the responsibility.

You can choose to have weight piled onto your shoulders or willingly pick up weight and charge forward. The difference between the two options is a philosophical one, yet a potent philosophy, nonetheless. You see, when we choose of our own free will to take on more challenges and accept more responsibility, we find ourselves feeling braver. Often, through the act of taking on more responsibility, we tend to discover that we *can* cope with it, this often creates a domino effect where our self-esteem will grow, and our sense of capability increases. This is very different from being *forced* to do something, as in this case, we find that we often cannot let go of the idea we were not ready and will proactively search for things that aren't "good enough," further making us feel incapable; Even if we do accept we were ready, we can easily make the mistake now of viewing our responsibilities as burdens rather than challenges. Things that we must "deal" with rather than things we can do.

Toward that end, we will be investigating a different form of archetyping known as life planning. In the previous chapter, I said that the method of archetyping can be adapted to a myriad of purposes. Here, we will be altering it heavily toward the purpose of building a life plan.

The principle no matter how you stretch or reshape it remains similar: First, We identify what we want; then, we seek to prioritize and categorize; lastly, we determine which relevant steps there are we can take that are actionable, easily measurable, and repeatable. In the end, what we are doing is taking some serious time to decide what we want — often putting in the effort of writing things down and pondering them — before deciding for ourselves that it will work. This is by far the best way you will ever hear of for self-discovery.

The nice thing about a life plan is that it gives us a firm grasp of where we are starting from and what we must do to reach new levels. Often when trying to take steps toward our future, we tend to forget to account in a realistic way for where we are now. The tragedy here is that you may endeavor to take on new goals in an overzealous manner, usually harboring far too many expectations of talent and speedy progress, and as a result, you will be needlessly cruel and unforgiving of your progress when you measure it. In fact, you will actually begin to convince yourself to give up before ever truly experiencing any success, often falling victim to the lie that you lack ability when in truth you actually did.

This is compounded by the fear of failure that I mentioned earlier. Whenever you endeavor to grow or develop an aspect of yourself you will first need to overcome an internal resistance to do it. This resistance will represent itself to you in a myriad of ways and can often only be identified by the outcome: an attempt *not* to do the thing you want to do. This is a self-defense mechanism we all have evolved into ourselves, you see; 5,000 years ago, if you grew up with a tribe that would *always* run away from bushes when they began to shake and rustle, this was often *always* the right thing to do.

Any individual who dared do something different and new from their usual patterns (aka, not run away from the bushes), often would be eaten by whatever was inside of the bushes. After having this truth harshly reinforced again and again over time, an inherent resistance to change has evolved into us as a part of our standard psychological wiring. Luckily, adaptability and willpower were also added in. Just because your mind is natively resistant to change, does not mean it always will be nor does it mean you have to obey it. You can acknowledge and accept this resistance for what it is, then endeavor to do the opposite regardless.

***

A life plan, therefore, becomes a tool that you can use to overcome many of your own worst tendencies and shortcomings, and can come with a host of benefits, all of which we will discuss in this section.

To start, the most powerful benefit of a life planner out there is its use as a tool with which to overcome our own fear of failure. By setting a series of objectives and reaching them, and understanding how they will guide you to a greater result, you will have far more motivation and internal strength to get you there.

You see, when it comes to our own internal fears of doing something, we often internally struggle with one of two things. First — and most often — we will find ourselves fearing a new endeavor simply out of uncertainty of what people in our social circle will think or how they will react. You will usually almost always rather *not* open up the restaurant you always wanted, speak to the pretty girl from your class, or write the book you've wanted out of fear of what others may say in reaction; this includes your parents, your friends, and any passerby strangers.

Of course, this is natural, as humans are inherently social animals and your own evolutionary wiring toward accounting for the "social impact" is expected. That being said…it is miscalibrated. In modern times the acceptance of the tribe no longer matters, as the tribe barely hangs out anymore and spends their days in an office cubicle, online, or alone in their bedroom. The price of failure is far lower, as whatever death is to be encountered from social isolation has been managed by medicine and technology. This means that for the most part, this fear should be ignored as much as is reasonable, especially if it holds you back from trying new things.

I must however warn you that your instincts are razor sharp and honed after many millennia of trial and error, usually when your gut warns you of something: it is true. However, the "intensity" of the concern is often something that should be accounted for. Often a fear of death is imposed on talking to the pretty girl/guy you've been eyeing, yet in truth even if everything goes wrong you'll only be a laughing stock for a max of 10 minutes before life goes on, people forget, and you will mostly be left unscathed. Sure, your pride may be a little hurt. But if you can prevent yourself from taking the shame to heart and beating yourself up about it you'll move on as if nothing happened.

Second, we tend to fear what a failure may "imply" about us. This is not an evolutionary trait, but rather a cultural one. You see, modern movies often portray characters that are unique, special, and talented right out of the box and inherently designed to be loved. Often, they are perfect and display a variety of talents and skills without ever putting in any effort to obtain them. This leads to an awkward situation where several generations of people are raised under the illusion that this is normal. There are several tragic outcomes to this, the first being reflected in a culture under the newer generations that each person is special — that this makes each of us perfect — and that it should be catered to. Altogether leading to many of the pitfalls of modern ideology we see today and much of the political infighting we see on social media. Although it is true that people are different, the truth is society should not cater to these differences. Instead, we should use our differences to *cater to society*; as we have a responsibility to understand who we are, what our talents and passions may be, and find a place for ourselves where we can serve others and build value happily.

The second outcome of our warped culture is actually quite dangerous for us, especially as we attempt to build healthy lives for ourselves. As mentioned, since people live under the illusion that it is normal to be "perfect right out of the box," the inherent fear develops that any failures or shortcomings are somehow proof of our inadequacy. We will often not chase many of our dreams, because we can't imagine who we would be if those dreams go "poof" in our faces. We can't imagine ourselves as successful when our heroes on TV and Instagram never seem to struggle, fail, and error like we do. This is a tragedy because we have accidentally created a culture where the act of failure becomes proof of incompetence, rather than a chance to grow (which is what failure actually is).

To make matters worse, we even went so far as to compound the effect by creating a culture where it is acceptable to slander people or even outright "cancel" them publicly on social media just for making a mistake. Often employees or even entire companies can be the target of a toxic culture that seeks to guillotine and annihilate them for a mistake in philosophy, conduct, or thinking. A better world existed not too long ago where people could make mistakes, be forgiven by friends and family, and provide ample opportunity to grow. These same people who humiliated themselves publicly and probably behaved and spoke in an abhorrent manner often grow into supremely wise mentors because they were given a chance to move on.

That time has faded, and in its place: we find people who are too paralyzed to make a mistake for fear of persecution, and when they do make mistakes it becomes a collar that they carry with them wherever they go. Of course, these external forces become internal barriers, as the idea that an act of imperfect behavior is proof of internal rot has taken root within our hearts and minds as a unique cancer among the young. The world is now filled with young men and women who have more proof that there is something wrong with them than proof that they are worthwhile and to be admired.

I therefore call for you to be brave.

It is not enough to declare the forces of our external culture as "illusions" and ignore them, often we will find our courage stolen when we feel that these false illusions carry weight.

It is often terrifying when what was thought to be a shadow grabs your leg.

Instead. Let us acknowledge these cultural forces for what they are: A problem. A problem and a challenge. We must accept their existence in order to move beyond them.

Luckily, this way, by knowing the issue and that it lies on the outside as well as within, we can seek to be truly brave and overcome it. We owe it to our own happiness to accept that failure is not an issue. We owe it to ourselves not to fear being mocked on social media or judged for having different tastes. We must be brave and do the things we know are right and be willing to fail again and again in pursuit of our own yearnings for a better life. To this end, we will begin to plan our lives in a way that contains a series of goals we can reach. We will often fail severely as we strive for them, yet in so doing, you will come to learn that failure is simply a part of the process. Then, regardless of if your fear is instinctive, cultural, or internalized, you will come to master it.

This is the key feature of using a life planner strategy, it allows us to ignore the complicated reality of life and break our dreams and aspirations down into a series of more manageable tasks. As we endeavor to complete these tasks, we often uncover the answers to all our unknown questions about ourselves and we improve our lives in the process.

Of course, it helps a ton that you will soon be breaking down your dreams into a series of manageable steps with our life planner. As there are more benefits beyond the management of fear. For one, a life planner will help us set our priorities and make better decisions.

This is important because one of the earliest lessons a person begins to learn in adulthood is that effectively nothing goes according to plan. When you go about your business of trying to achieve your goals you will consistently be thrown off course by all forms of other influence within life. At this point, having a good life planner will help you remember what it is you are actually trying to achieve and be more effective at making new plans.

There is a new saying that has been floating around recently, the source of which I am not certain: "Set your goals in stone and make your plans in the sand." A statement that is most astute to anyone wanting to make something of their lives. Very often you will wake up with the goal of achieving various tasks in your day only to find that the day takes you in a new direction, and you are forced to make decisions on what to prioritize and how to go about achieving your goals in new ways. Hilariously enough though, the same thing will happen no matter the time scale we use or the degree of difficulty we set our goals. If you want to achieve something with your week, the same problem. If you want to spend the next three months working toward something, again, the same problem. Life will derail you and the three months could go by without you ever realizing that you aren't taking a step toward your goal. A life plan counters this by giving a simple reminder.

Finally, a life planner will give you a better sense of control over the various facets of your life and give you a sense of empowerment and motivation. As mentioned earlier, movies and social media have indulged the mass cultural delusion that people can be inherently perfect as a character trait. Meaning that we often think people can be perfectly motivated, yet this couldn't be further from the truth. The truth is that for all people on earth, the act of staying motivated is a constant game of managing your energy and talking positively to yourself. Choosing to see value and meaning in your actions rather than seeing meaninglessness or a waste of time and energy.

Remember, this truth accounts for all people.

That means it is applicable to even the most high-performing people out there as well as our most admired athletes, CEOs, influencers, and celebrities. For all of these people, the rule is the same, they have no choice but to manage their own energy and motivation toward a goal. This is not something you are born with, it is a skill you train.

The fantastic news here is that even the most unmotivated, uncoordinated, lazy, and tired among us can uplift themselves with effort and practice. It all boils down to self-talk and how you choose to look at your efforts.

At its core, it's about how you choose to experience the things you do.

For every action you take or event you experience, there exists a choice to seek some value in it and try to feel some excitement or gratitude; or lament and flagellate yourself in anguish as you rue your actions and hate yourself.

Let's say for example that you need to study for a math test. The situation is quite dire, as you often never get above a D for all your past math tests, and you, as well as your lecturer/teacher, are convinced that you will fail the test and fail the year. At this point, the wisdom of the weak is to accept you may not be good at math and change your majors to a more "accepting" role. Or, you could try and grasp your dreams and face the challenge. If you find the act of practicing math mind gnawingly awful, then make it exciting. Go buy a whiteboard, put on some music that forces you to feel engaged, and spend hours in front of the whiteboard practicing your stuff.

It sounds silly, but putting in a little effort to make your chores and labors a little more engaging and positive has a major impact on the outcome. Any fool can sit at a desk, do the math homework they hate, and gripe to themselves about how awful it is. In fact, so many fools do it that few people actually reach a point where they learn that math can be enjoyable once you get good at it. This is why your teacher/lecturer may assume your failure, they've seen thousands before you moan as they sat down to practice, and with time they came to accept the pattern.

The pattern is a simple one: What you tell yourself becomes your truth. If you tell yourself you hate math as well as exclaim it to all those around you. It will be your reality. You will hate doing it. However, if you force yourself to try and admire the math, as well as enjoy your own efforts in pursuing it, then you will eventually find yourself enjoying it. Granted, it will take some time, it always does; but as long as you keep faking it, you'll eventually make it. In this way, using a life planner is a good way to make yourself feel more engaged with your attempts to motivate yourself, as you are trying to actively exercise a muscle you probably never used before, and that may need an external tool to keep you going.

*** 

As mentioned, a core part of setting up a life plan is recognizing that it is effectively a form of archetyping as well. You need to start with a vision of where you want to be and use it to set a long-term goal. Let's pretend it truly is your dream to be a famous YouTuber or social media influencer. You will need to start by doing some research and estimating how many followers/subscribers you will need before your account/channel starts earning the money you like. For Instagram, the minimum needed to monetize your account will be roughly 1,000 followers and for YouTube, it will be 1,000 subscribers. We therefore have our first goals, which you should go write down in a journal.

(Note: Please write your own goals, not the example above…it would be silly of you to write down the goals I outlined in my example above on becoming an influencer. Unless you actually *do* want to become an influencer…)

Now that we have written down our five goals, let's continue by taking note of where we are now, and asking ourselves what we are doing now. In the next step of the exercise, I want you to write down all the actions you took in the past week that contributed to reaching your goals, as shown in the subsequent image.

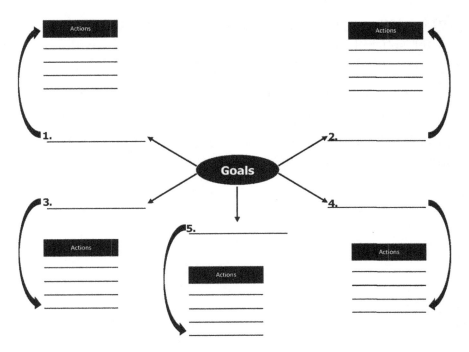

You may notice in doing so that you may have done very little that actually contributed to your goal. Why? This is an important question. Perhaps you always find yourself distracted by something. Perhaps other chores or responsibilities keep getting in the way. We cannot be certain of any of this, but what we can do is write down what the obstacles/distractions/burdens were that stopped us from getting where we want to go. For some people, they may find that they did virtually nothing to reach their goals. Again, the task before you is *why*. Very often, this is because we fail to recognize small efforts as efforts. Taking the time to take a picture for your account, or read up on the moves of other influencers actually counts toward your goals; albeit only a little bit...other than that, this may be a matter of motivation. You must ask yourself why you may be stopping yourself from attaining your dreams and spend some time reinforcing better self-talk and enjoyment of your passion. In the case of our influencer example; let's say that very little content creation was done because we don't have an adequate environment to record inside our homes and our university studies are getting in the way. So let's write this all down, as shown next:

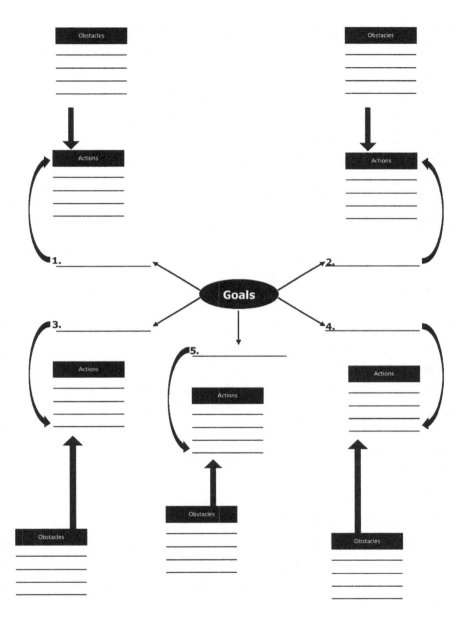

Now, we've arrived at a junction where we know what we want, we know what we are doing to get there, and we even pondered what is stopping us from getting there. You may think the next step is to go and find solutions, but no, sometimes the obstacles we described above are actually a reflection of our own responsibilities. This is where most people go wrong, once again, due to the influence of movie writing and social media culture. The pursuit of your dreams and inner fulfillment should always take priority, but never beyond that of your direct responsibilities as an adult. In our above example, perhaps university studies are getting in the way because you've been neglectful of them and had to spend a lot of your time catching up this past week or just "coping." The solution is not to drop out of Uni in pursuit of your dreams of becoming an influencer, but rather to focus on your studies, ensuring you work ahead and that you feel comfortable first before you begin to tackle your passions.

We can find another example if we pretend that you've been skipping the registrations of your car, have a court date for a speeding ticket, and your driver's license has also recently expired. These are all things that accumulate and build up as you go about life, inadvertently neglecting your responsibilities toward owning and maintaining a vehicle. Ignoring them may seem an easy choice, I mean how often does any of the "bureaucracy" of car ownership really affect your day-to-day life? Well, if the judge sees you've been neglecting your duties as a member of society (yes, this is a thing) then you may find yourself saddled with a $500 dollar court fine. Perhaps you could get lucky and have your social media blow up when you post about this, earning 50K followers in a week as a video of your fine and subsequent tantrum goes viral, yet your first $500 paycheck may very well go directly toward paying this off.

Perhaps it's far wiser to take care of your business first and earn those 50K followers later in a more sensible way?

Therefore, the next step in our creation of a life plan is to account for how many of our obstacles are actually responsibilities and write them down below as well as a revised list of obstacles. Also, be aware you may have responsibilities that are indirectly hindering you or adding to the pressure of an obstacle, write those down where applicable. You'll likely notice that only a handful of obstacles and responsibilities at this point are holding you back:

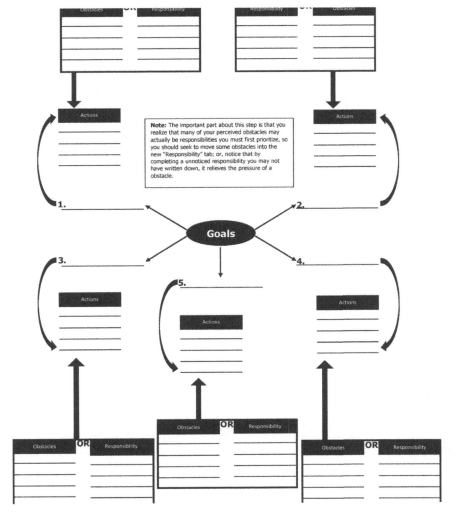

Now we get to the good part, as next, you need to go back to the observations you made on the actions you take toward your goal, and compare it to their outcomes. Ask yourself honestly, how much closer are you to reaching your target? Did the things I do contribute, and in which way? When will I get to my goal? Find ways to improve your current actions and write them down, as shown in the subsequent example:

## Improvement of Outcomes

Which actions have I been performing to reach my goals?

_____

_____

_____

_____

_____

_____

_____

_____

_____

_____

What outcomes have I been experiencing? Is it good enough?

When will I reach my goals?

_____

_____

_____

_____

_____

_____

How can we go about improving the actions we've been taking to make them more effective?

_____

_____

_____

_____

_____

Ultimately, the core reason for the previous exercise is to assist you in generating a list of reasonable, repeatable, tasks that you can perform each day. Thus, Now we get to the core purpose of the whole series of past exercises, as now we need to ask ourselves:

What should I be doing differently? What do I need to do next? What should I prioritize? You must ask these questions and generate a list of tasks. Preferably repeatable tasks. That you can write down and use later to guide yourself more toward your goals. Same as in archetyping, the key is not to write down vague or abstract actions like "be more mindful" or "use time sparingly."

Rather, you want a list of tasks that can be easily tracked and measured. Often with a yes/no outcome or quantitative way of measuring. If you want to be more mindful, task yourself to meditate for 10 minutes. If you want to be more aware of your use of time, set a timer whenever you sit down to work and use it to regulate and track your usage of your own time. Complete the exercise as shown on the succeeding image:

## Task List Generation

What should I be doing differently? What do I need to do next?

_____
_____
_____
_____
_____

What goals should I prioritize?

_____
_____
_____
_____
_____
_____
_____

Which easily repeatable, measurable, tasks can I perform to reach my goals?

_____
_____
_____
_____
_____
_____
_____
_____
_____
_____

Up till now we've been asking questions to ourselves and accumulating information. Much like how we discussed in our archetyping section, this is in no way a one-time thing, nor is it set in stone. If you are smart, you will be going through this exercise several times in your life, perhaps even a few times in the coming year.

The reason why is because we as people are far less set in stone than we like to think. All aspects of ourselves, ranging from our personalities, our beliefs, and our outlooks exist in a constant state of flux, with the only constant being the patterns you use in your day-to-day. If you are a young 16-year-old or perhaps even a 22-year-old reading this, I cannot even begin to describe to you how different of a person you will be in 5 years' time. To be frank, you'll probably be a little different by the end of the year, especially if it was an eventful year. This is why I actually recommend doing both the archetyping exercise as well as the life planner exercise several times throughout the next few years, as each time you do it, it will help orient you a bit.

Of course, we aren't done yet. There is still one more task we need to do, and this is to set up a proper intention journal. This is the end result of our whole exercise, as well as the efforts in our previous archetyping chapter. Here, our goal is simply to create a small journal we can keep beside our bed that we will use to guide us forward into the future. An intention journal serves as our compass to move into the storms of fear and avoid the distractions that life will throw at us. If you go do some further reading about this online you will notice my approach is a bit more in-depth than intention journaling, however, I can assure you it is more secure and constant. Furthermore, research has shown that maintaining an intention journal improves your ability to achieve your goals significantly.

So, first let's orient ourselves and actually make use of all the exercises you've been doing. We should start by creating a list of our main responsibilities, then we write down our daily tasks that we've recently identified as being vital for reaching our goals, and afterward, we write down our common obstacles. We already generated and evaluated all this information in previous exercises; now you must write these down for yourself in your journal, and if you want, you can do it how I like to:

## Intention Journal First Page

**Responsibilities:**

**Tasks:**

**Obstacles:**

**Solutions:**

This list will act as the first page of our intention journal, and I wish for you to add it in whatever way you like into the first page of a small journal book. This book will be your intention journal.

This is how an intention journal works: Each day when you wake up the first thing you do is take the intention journal and consult your list. You need to select two responsibilities (university, work, taxes, kids, pets, chores, etc.) that you made for yourself and decide which will get your attention today. The number of responsibilities you choose is somewhat dependent on the life you live. If you are a 25-year-old mom who studies at a university, then your responsibilities will automatically boil down to kids and university, and you will probably have to go up to three or four responsibilities depending on how involved the other parent is in maintaining a home. Likewise, if you're a 16-year-old kid, your responsibilities may consist only of school and perhaps even chores. I'd say set your range from two to four responsibilities. You will write these down and set them as priorities for the day.

Now, the thing about responsibilities is that often we cannot "set them aside." No matter which you choose, the chances are good you may still need to "maintain" the others. However, by choosing two to four responsibilities we are actually saying to ourselves: "This deserves extra focus for today." For example, if you have kids and you chose them, then perhaps make a point of sitting down with them and doing homework or at least having a chat. Perhaps there is a parent-teacher day later that day, or a sports game you need to attend, in which case you will automatically be choosing this responsibility for the day.

Then, depending on what you chose, look at your desired tasks (the ones that build toward your goals) and choose one to three of them that you think you can manage that day. Obviously, your decision will depend on how you plan on squeezing them into your day. Doing a 10-minute meditation is one thing, but spending two or three hours researching your competition for a business venture is another. So at this stage, it is more important to simply find something for you to do that day that fits into your day than forcing yourself to choose three of them.

Then, consult your obstacles list and choose the obstacles that will most likely challenge your day. Write all the ones you think may be relevant to your day. Perhaps all of your obstacles will be a challenge today, perhaps only one. The important part is that once they are chosen, you write a solution for each one. If you think motivation will be an obstacle, then a solution may be positive self-talk (Or from my prior math example, a whiteboard, and some music). Likewise, if you worry about time management consider the use of timers and alarms to force yourself to be aware of its passage. The important part is that each obstacle has its own custom solution. The nice thing about asking yourself to think of new solutions each day for common obstacles is that eventually you will find a few that always work well, and a few that work under certain situations.

Write down your completed list of responsibilities, bonus tasks, and obstacles/solutions for the day in the journal. These will be your "intentions" for the day. Obviously, we can at this point be certain things will not go according to plan. However, since you took the time to remember your responsibilities, your aspirations, and crash course solutions to your problems, you may find your day being more productive and meaningful regardless of all the plans going out the window. When the day is over, go back to today's page in the intention journal and take a moment to check off each item you successfully tackled that day. It does not matter that you did it perfectly, nor that you did the task to completion. The important part lies in your attempt to do them, and your acknowledgment of your efforts thereafter. You can also write a paragraph at the end of the list to note some observations or future solutions to yourself. I'd also recommend taking a moment to feel grateful for your efforts, especially if you didn't feel your efforts were valued throughout the day (which is often the case for almost all adults, as our efforts to do things are often not acknowledged).

When you do all this journaling in this specific way, you're actually creating a ton of subconscious feedback and forcing yourself to form positive habits, which with time snowballs into the creation of a lean-mean hustler who operates at a very high level. Eventually allowing you to ditch the book.

Note: In the next chapter I will be giving you an exercise page that you can use within your intention journal. You need not use it, however, I think it will do you good if you try, as it comes from my *Pantheria Life Log* and is more mindful of your core Maslow hierarchy needs.

★ ★ ★ ★ ★

# Your Feedback Counts

## Please, leave a REVIEW
## wherever you made your purchase.

Share your experience with
others help us grow our audience.

 Booksprout

**For the opportunity to read advanced copies of our
books, join our review team on BookSprout:**

**https://booksprout.co/reviewer/team/
31264/panterax-book-review-team**

# MANAGING
# YOUR RESOURCES

In the year 281 BC, king Pyrrhus of Epirus received a request for aid from across the ionic sea that a Greek colony, the city of Tarentum, was under threat of invasion from the Roman legionaries after their continuous expansion into Greek territories. The Romans had already plundered the city of Tarentum once and diplomatic talks with greater Greece were going downhill. Feeling indebted to the colony for their assistance in past wars, and being close to Macedonia with the legends of Alexander the Great still hanging fresh in the hearts of many; he fancied a similar legend of conquest and greatness for himself and began to bolster a narrative among his allies and men of his coming reunification of the Macedonia that was lost in 285 BC. Having no wealth to do this, he contacted all his allies in an attempt to muster a great army, promising riches from the plunder of Rome and conquest of the west. He reached out to the current ruler of Macedonia, Egypt, as well as Greece, as he bolstered an army of roughly 25,000 to 30,000, consisting of war elephants, archers, spearmen, and cavalry. The bulk of his men consisted of the Macedonian phalanx infantry—a professional contingent of Greek soldiers whose battle doctrine and use of the "phalanx" were made famous by Alexander the Great himself in his conquest of the world.

This force was a large one, yet compared to the Romans it was actually a lot smaller, as the Romans had mustered a force of 80,000 men of Roman auxiliary who had been divided into four armies in preparation for his conquest. King Pyrrhus was aware of the larger force he faced, yet he knew the quality and power of his troops were the best from all corners of the earth and were far greater when compared to the masses of Roman auxiliaries who relied on discipline and formation alone, rather than skill and lifelong training, to win their wars.

His force was by far the most "elite," with its soldiers fiercely trained from a young age, defined only as true warriors. In the eyes of all who watched—kings, empires, tribes, and cities—this would be a clash between all of Rome's strength and the might of Greece's past legends. In the year 280 BC, he sailed across the sea with his force of "elite" troops and elephant cavalry to save the city of Tarentum from the endless masses of Romans, reunify the Macedonian Empire, restore the position of Greece as a world power, and solidify his legend as a successor to Alexander the Great. He already had received pledges of support and loyalty from various local tribes and Greek cities, and merely had to get the ball rolling.

His arrival at the shores of Tarentum in 280 BC would herald the initial casting of cement that would later be his legacy as the founder of the term "Pyrrhic victory," a term reserved solely for the act of losing because of "how" you won. You see, King Pyrrhus would spend a long time in the city of Tarentum waiting for reinforcements that would never come. This was because two of the aforementioned Roman armies had moved into key territories for the purpose of blocking any uprisings from the recently quelled tribes as well as preventing further Greek reinforcements from bolstering Pyrrhus's army.

King Pyrrhus was clever enough to eventually realize the reinforcements of the local people would never come, and advanced on the city of Heraclea where the other two Roman armies were positioned. King Pyrrhus was a good tactician and made a body-double wear his armor as he donned a normal soldier's armor himself. Furthermore, he took a superior position behind the river Siris (now Sinni) and kept his elephant cavalry hidden in reserve — away from Roman eyes who had never seen such beasts before — to make himself appear weak.

When the Romans attacked the battle was fierce. The unstoppable Roman legions had crashed into the unbreakable Greek phalanx — which 200 years earlier had fought limitless Persian advances under the guidance of the Spartans and King Leonidas — and the number of Romans was truly staggering, yet the Greek troops held the line; until they began to lose heart when his body double was killed, fearing that the king had in fact died.

King Pyrrhus was able to rally his troops by removing his helmet and moving to the front line, cheering his men on as he rode his horse past their battle lines, so that they could see he still lived. His soldiers were bolstered by the act of bravery and began to fight back the Roman legions with increased ferocity, at this point, King Pyrrhus ordered his elephants to attack a unit of Roman cavalry who had been harassing his flanks. The elephants overwhelmed the enemy cavalry before advancing on the main Roman force.

The appearance of these giant animals who had firing towers full of troops on their backs terrified the Roman legionaries who had never seen such creatures before.

They began to retreat across the river at which point King Pyrrhus' army chased them down and killed many of them. The Roman losses were staggering, and many prisoners were taken. The king advanced his men beyond the river into the city of Heraclea where he again defeated yet another Roman army using a similar combination of foresight, intuition, and clever tactics. Yet with such victory about him, the king found himself having lost much. You see, he had lost as many as 7,500 troops during these battles, as well as many of his elephants. Although he still had an army to spare, the Romans still had two large armies preventing him from reinforcing locally and the men he had lost were some of his most elite fighters as well as most of his officers. What remained were among the weaker and more cowardly of his men, who although still capable of fighting, had lost much heart seeing their stronger brothers fall in battle, and the belief of the "rebirth" of king Alexander the Great had left them along with the souls of their commanders.

This was a phenomenon that would come to define his attempted conquest of Rome. King Pyrrhus was clever and still tried to keep fighting his war for five more years. Each victory was hard fought and often came at staggering costs, and King Pyrrhus exhausted all his intellect and guile to achieve each victory against the endless Roman legions. The ancient historian Plutarch quoted him saying that: "If we are victorious in one more battle against the Romans, we will be utterly ruined." In the year 275 BC, a setback in the Battle of Beneventum convinced him to call off his invasion and head home.

After five years of near constant victory, he returned home empty-handed.

This moment in history serves as a clear example of what a "Pyrrhic victory" is, and has since then been studied by historians and military commanders alike so that they can avoid doing much of the same. You see, often in life, it happens far too easily where one can expend a massive amount of effort, time, energy, and money only to walk home with, well…not enough to show for it.

A victory is achieved and there is indeed something gained, yet the cost is often so great it nullifies whatever value can be gleaned from it.

History is often filled with many people achieving pyrrhic victories, one such example is the tale of Lance Armstrong, the only man ever to win seven tours de France tours by constructing the most elaborate and intricate steroid doping conspiracy in sports history, only to be stripped of all titles, sponsorships, and accolades when inevitably caught doping anyway.

Many further examples are found commonly in the Pacific war against the Japanese, where the American navy often gained ground through the immense cost of human life and resources (ultimately culminating in the decision to drop the atomic bomb). Yet even still, the most common and blatant Pyrrhic victory we all see every day lies in the decision of many young people to go and study for a degree, "because it's what people do after school."

You see, for the most part, I consider the act of getting a degree at a young age a Pyrrhic victory in and of itself. One of the most common trends of the modern era is seeing a slew of young 21-year-olds posting pictures of their graduation photos, only to see them post memes shortly thereafter about the burdens of student debt and how "employers want

5-years experience as well as a degree," even though no one has 5-years experience after graduation.

Now don't get me wrong, there is indeed a student debt crisis in America, and it can undoubtedly feel unjust that you should spend several years of your youth pursuing and bleeding for a piece of paper that *still* doesn't fully qualify you for a job. These arguments are undoubtedly valid. I also don't want you standing up from your chair, calling your parents, and declaring with childlike certainty, "I'm dropping out."

I just want you to think about something.

How do you know what you want to do?

If you are a 16 or 18-year-old kid lying in your bed reading this book, or even a 20-year-old, and you try to convince me you know "exactly" what you want to do with your life, I won't believe you.

I can assure you, there's a good 60 to 70% chance you will change your mind in 6 years' time. I'm not trying to attack your beliefs or passions here, I'm simply stating a fact: most young people have no clue what they want to do, even when they think they do. Chances are good that if you're reading this and you are below the age of 25, you will be doing something other than what you were planning to do by the turn of your 30s. Go talk to your parents or other "adults" in your life, most will have changed careers or professions several times before settling in somewhere. There do exist many exceptions to this rule as many won't be changing careers, but for the most part, they will be the minority. In my own case, I spent the greater part of a decade in my 20s trying to start a record label while trying to work several jobs. Although it never took off, by the end of it I knew what I should do next and after some studies, I became an IT technician for the US navy.

I want a similar experience for you. I think one of the best ways a young 20-year-old can spend their time is by doing all sorts of jobs and exploring what brings them a sense of fulfillment in life. This way, when you make the decision to study for a degree in your mid to late 20s, you'll know exactly what to do next and do a lot better in the degree. I know this is a bit off the beaten path, but I can assure you that in my own experience it was quite worth it to experience a wide plateau of work avenues and taste a variety of challenges, as it allowed me to be more assured in my choice of study and specialization later in life, it also prevented the sticky situation where I wouldn't need 5-years work experience fresh out of college, as I already had 5 years work experience by that point.

This boils down to a bit of a personal philosophy I have about the various stages of life. When I look over my past life I would say there are roughly four stages.

The first stage occurs between the ages of 0-25. For the most part, the events here are beyond your control, and when you turn 18 you are treated like an adult even though it can be fully recognized by everyone that your mind still needs a few years of development before it reaches its peak. For those who don't know, the mind is still developing well into 25, and that's why most people under 25 are still somewhat treated like kids by society. We can all see it and know it's true, and when you reach that age you'll notice it also. If you are in this stage, I'd recommend fully exploring as many careers and passions as you possibly can. At this point in your life, you probably have no responsibilities and plenty of energy, so it is an ideal opportunity to explore your strengths and weaknesses and perhaps even earn some money and things to write down on a CV. If there is anything you should avoid here, it would be getting stuck. Don't get stuck working a dead-end job for chump change unless it somehow benefits you long term. Don't wind up studying a degree in accounting and racking up debt when a part of you *knows* you don't want to do accounting. Don't get pregnant. If you happen to do *any* of these things, make the most of it. Even if you wind up stuck somewhere, your life is long, and you never know where you'll be in 5 years. Try to enjoy it and keep finding ways to "build" something, even if it is something small and silly.

The second stage of your life in my opinion occurs between the age of 25 to 50, with most of the action hopefully occurring before you are 40. You see, roughly at about the age of 26 the idea is that you would have acquired enough knowledge and experience about your own desires, talents, abilities, and capabilities that you should have some clue of where you will be able to fit into society. Here is a moment where you can commit to building a life for yourself. There are steps and goals here you should try to adhere to.

Step 1: Identify a societal role suited for you and try to specialize in it. This means taking the time to realize you wished you were an accountant, get a loan to study, and become an accountant.

Step 2 is the most important: Gain 10 years of experience in whatever you want to do so that you can build social circles and recognition as a professional. This is key. Much of people's success, especially later in life, hinges on having some sort of reputation that can be backed or acknowledged by other players in an industry. One day when you are older, your status as an X (doctor, manager, accountant, IT consultant, businessman, realtor, lawyer, etc.) will simply open doors for you that would have otherwise required hours of grinding and imagination to reach when you were younger. Take a look at Donald Trump, much of his ability to have become a president rested on the reputation and image as a businessman he had built up on TV in the years preceding his race to the office. Whether or not you think this reputation was good or bad becomes irrelevant, as the reputation alone; was all he needed to take a jump. It's a terrifying prospect, really; the truth is, the moment you establish a name or brand for yourself, good or bad, it can open doors. That is why it becomes your goal no matter what to choose an industry, specialize in it, and aim to gather at least 10 years of experience. That way, you would have built up a softer world for yourself during the second half of your life.

Step 3 is a matter of reward. Having specialized in an industry and having built a reputation, seek to spend the ending half of your 40s reaping the rewards thereof, whatever it may be. If there is a promotion to a cushy job in sight, chase it. If you didn't get the job, apply for a higher position elsewhere and establish yourself in a new firm. If you were smart enough to make a few investments, consider cashing them out. At the very least, seek to have a property or two paid off at this point. Our goal as this phase of our life closes off is to have a secure series of assets that can be used to keep you safe in the later years.

The third stage of your life constitutes the stage where your earnings potential should be maximized, and starts at the age of 50 and I'd say it will last roughly into the age of 75. Although you will be earning your maximum here and likely are well versed in one or two professions, your goal in this stage is to take some time archetyping and planning your life ahead, perhaps occasionally taking a hard-earned deep breath. Ideally, you want to be setting everything up so that you won't be needing to work later. It may be easy to assume this is old age, but these days medicine and living standards keep people alive well into their 90s. For the most part, at this point, you would have achieved most of the goals you set out in your life.

The final stage starts at 75, and is a test. You should have saved up enough at this point and made enough plans that your income should be a lot more than a Social Security check each month. Preferably, at this point, any work you do should be a choice and most of your efforts should be geared toward what you leave behind. This is the time you spend with grandkids and leaving something behind for others.

Now, having discussed the various life stages, let's take some time to return to the topic at hand, which is the avoidance of a pyrrhic victory. Here, it becomes important to understand that most things worth doing in life, including chasing your passions, require effort. If you don't take the time to plan and manage your efforts even your most savored pleasures and pastimes can become a major chore that suffocates you. The trick is to realize that the moment you decide to work hard at something, you'll enjoy it less; and that's okay.

No really, It's okay. It's normal.

This is a mistake I see young people making all the time, they go about the world avoiding any and all jobs that have a 40-hour work week citing that it is toxic and will suffocate them, arguing that they'd rather chase something they enjoy and are passionate about. This is all well and dandy, and I even agree; that you *should* do that which you are passionate about...but please come to terms with the fact that when you embark on this, no matter what it is, a lot of it will require mind-numbing work that you will hate! Very often, it may even require you to work well over 40 hours in a quest to complete it. I, therefore, weep whenever I see legions of people sitting on their hands, waiting for something "fun" to land on their laps, assuming that when it happens it will be a sign that they have found the thing they've always wanted to do, exclaiming: "This is my passion! This is my purpose! It's so fun it won't feel like work at all!"

Not at all, people who do this simply wind up far behind the rest of us before realizing — like the rest of us, and one day you — that instead of waiting for their passions to arrive they should have rather diligently chased after its shadow. Because that way they would have eventually caught a glimmer of fulfillment, or at least a glimpse of what it is that makes them happy in life, to begin with.

This harkens back to many of my own past experiences when I was trying to start a record company. I ended up working 40-hour weeks trying to gather all the money I could, simply to sink it into my company. Me and a few friends were working together to do this, and we poured all our collective efforts together for the sake of achieving one thing:

Quality.

Above all else, the tracks we recorded had to be of the highest quality, and this required thousands of dollars at all times. My pursuit of this passion was indeed labor, and in doing it I had a chance to grasp how the world works and reach for something higher. At the height of our efforts, me and my partners were visiting record stores, attending industry events, and networking with various radio stations on a weekly basis—this was in between working full-time jobs, all of us. It took three years of hard effort for me and my partners to raise the company up to the point where we were releasing quality content on a regular basis, and I'm sure if we kept at that pace for two more years, we'd have had a breakthrough.

Unfortunately, after a while me and my partners began to have disagreements and we split up, leading to the downfall of the company. Admittedly, we never had a chance to reach our full potential and for the most part, we didn't get a lot of airing time on our songs; but a radio station did have a "Dig it, or Ditch it" event where they would play "underground" songs and people would vote on if it was good or not. Three of our songs wound up there, and all three of them were voted to be fantastic songs by the audience. I believe this happened due to the high-quality standards we maintained at all times with our artists and track production.

The purpose of that story is to convey how much effort your passions will actually require, and where they may end if the dice is rolled against your favor. This is not meant to dissuade you, this is meant to teach you the *minimum* you need to be willing to put down if you want to chase your dreams. You see, when I was chasing my dream it was hard, grueling, work. It took a while to adjust to and maintain the pressure, but in the end, it was worth it as I came to learn my limits; I was proud. I was proud of how much I could achieve when I took control of myself, and I loved the feeling that accompanied it. I was tired, and I was happy. This is a fate I would wish for anyone willing to discover themselves.

So we thus reach a bit of a paradox. On the one hand, we find through the trials of King Pyrrhus that we must avoid wasting our efforts; on the other, we see that large volumes of effort are the bare minimum needed when in pursuit of our dreams and trying to build a future. Our great challenge, and the purpose of this chapter, is to define and label the thin line between wasting our energy and doing more than enough.

To start, it should be said that a plethora of texts has been written on the topic of controlling and planning the use of your energy. Discussing them all now would be nearly impossible, and I imagine many of them would be contradictory. Therefore, let us take the wiser approach of first broadly discussing two main schools of thought regarding the matter. First, there is the ideology that we should be more mindful of where we expend our energy. Second, there is the notion that we should gear our efforts more toward the cultivation of our energy.

Now, whenever people discuss the matter of "energy" our minds begin to collectively meander in various different directions. Some will make the association with "vitality," concluding that when we speak of energy we speak of our "can do" attitude. Others will draw a link toward focus and concentration, and yet even more people will start to think of good vs. bad emotions as a parallel between high and low energy. The reason why this happens is that, by intent, the term energy actually broadly refers to most of these things. The truth is that the human experience can be so vast, that a need exists for us to refer to energy in such a broad manner. Yet in the end, we can still try and narrow it down a bit. For the context of this book, energy will refer to your "willingness" to listen when you try and motivate yourself to do stuff. It will refer to your willpower and your tendency to obey and enforce your own will. Which I think is a definition that encapsulates most of the other outlooks for energy.

The first approach is by far the easiest to master, as the idea is that you should take the time to notice what saps your energy. Once you know, you need to overcome whatever internal barrier you face or find a way to cleverly avoid it. Let's say, for example, that when you sit down to work you become overwhelmed with stress, and this forces you to stand up and do something else. Perhaps it even pushes you to open a video game instead of those dreaded excel spreadsheets. Well...this would be a clear example of an energy-sapping event, as it would require some willpower to force yourself to sit and work. I, therefore, recommend you jot it down. With time, as you record more things that will drain your energy, you'll come to notice some patterns and even make peace with your own ability to overcome them.

The second approach is a matter of generating energy. Many people associate this with "doing the things you are passionate about"; however, what they don't realize is that — although this will feed your energy — you'll often expend a lot of willpower getting to a point where your passions are rewarded. Recall my above story about my record label, it took a lot of grinding and time to get to a point where I was happy with it. Therefore, you need to take the time to appreciate the little things instead and try to generate the value of your efforts as you do them. This all harkens back to what I wrote earlier on learning what motivates you, however now, we are allowing a degree of self-discovery as we journey toward a scenario where we begin to acknowledge the little things that can bring us joy, like completing a small task or taking some time to experience gratitude.

In my case, I found a lot of value in managing my health a bit better and becoming aware of my underlying biology. You'd be surprised how big a difference it makes to spend an hour a day doing some exercise and eating well. When we exercise our bodies release all sorts of hormones that play a massive role in motivation and mood regulation. I know there are a lot of people out there who feel tired of hearing this sales gimmick repeated over-and-over verbatim, but I assure you the difference can be like night and day for some people after a week or two of regular exercise. In fact, I'd argue there are a lot of people out there facing all manner of emotional mountains, who would see them overcome had they chosen to exercise daily. We need to remember the modern lifestyle is an unnatural one; your body wasn't made to sit around all day, in fact, the entirety of its physiology and biology is geared toward walking and running around all the time, jumping and climbing, carrying heavy things, and eating a lot less than we do in modern times.

Talking about eating…your diet also plays a massive role in your mood. Foods that are packed full of vitamins, antioxidants, fiber, and starches play a major role in mood regulation. Again, I'm aware you've heard this a million times, but you must understand there is a reason why. Your body needs these chemicals to make hormones and regulate your mood. Is it really that hard to imagine that you may not be making any happy hormones because your body lacks the building materials? Foods like berries, oats, sweet potatoes, fruits, and vegetables can have a major impact on your body's ability to make you feel chipper. It can also be mentioned at this point that overeating can make you feel lethargic, and eating an abundance of fast food will make you pick up weight, which I can assure you will make you feel worse about yourself also.

Therefore, taking the time to manage your health tends to have a major impact on your daily happiness. One of the best ways to get out of a funk is to go for a run, or at least a long walk in a nice park. And I assure you, nothing will make you feel more motivated about life than feeling healthy. To assist in all this, I include a page from my other book; *Pantheria Life*

*Log,* which is a journal-style life planner I made full of tips and techniques I use to manage and gain control of my life. If having a life planner you can use to manage and record your progress sounds like a thing for you, I'd recommend having a look on Amazon.

On the page, you'll find an example from the *Pantheria Life Log* on how to write your goals and intentions for the day (as we discussed in the previous chapter), as well as various segments that seek to record things like water intake, mood, diet, health info, etc. You'll notice if you use this long enough that there can be a pattern between the foods you eat, exercise, locations, etc., and your mood. Knowing these things can help you claim some ownership of your life, as we are far more slaves to our bodies than we like to admit. You need not use the page for the rest of your life, just long enough to form the right habits and get going, which should be two months give or take. As a bonus, it acts as a great tool to realize just how many things you often accomplish on a daily basis, and can assist in feeling some gratitude.

**DATE**  ⬭  Ⓢ Ⓜ Ⓣ Ⓦ Ⓣ Ⓕ Ⓢ

## THINGS I'M GRATEFUL FOR

1. _____
2. _____
3. _____

## VITALS

| WEIGHT | BLOOD PRESSURE | HEART RATE |
|--------|----------------|------------|
|        |                |            |

## TODAYS EVENTS

_____
_____
_____
_____
_____
_____
_____
_____
_____
_____
_____
_____
_____
_____
_____
_____

## TODAY GOALS

☐ _____
☐ _____
☐ _____
☐ _____

## TASK AND NOTES

## TODAYS WINS

## TODAYS LESSONS

## MY LOCATION

## MEAL

| Breakfast | Lunch |
|-----------|-------|
| Dinner    | Snack |

**WATER INTAKE**  🜄🜄🜄🜄🜄🜄🜄🜄

**DAILY EXERCISE**

## TODAY I FEEL  😊 😌 😲 😠 😟

An example of the daily tasker/journal portion of the Pantheria Life Log.

***

So one of the first things you'll be doing when you move out of your parent's home is planning a budget. This is a vital first step to any adulthood, yet it walks hand-in-hand with a second all-important factor: Adhering to the budget. It can happen quite easily where a perfect budget is laid out, only to be thwarted when you decide to order a pizza.

The realm of budgeting is filled with many perils, and in order to circumvent the dangers that will accompany it, we will need to first inform ourselves of the mistakes others commonly make.

To start, Let us consider an underlying truth to what budgeting is. It is an attempt to achieve a goal. You won't simply go about counting pennies "because that's what adults do," you'll be counting pennies because you're saving up for a car, paying off a student loan, or buying a new computer — *that* is what adults do. Not understanding this crucial truth can lead to many pitfalls. For one, you may end up spreading yourself too thin; It may not be possible to save for a car *and* pay off your debt *and* save for a PC *and* save for a trip overseas. The fact is you will only have so much money to move around each month, so take the time to really consider what you want and commit to one goal. Furthermore, when not aligning your budget with long-term goals, you can easily make the common mistake of aligning them with someone else's goals. Very often, it happens that you may find yourself budgeting for a trip your friends insist you must join, yet this will require you to sacrifice your own financial dreams. Perhaps consider suggesting a cheaper trip or evaluating how much that vacation means to you. In fact, very often we find ourselves budgeting for an unsustainable lifestyle only so that we can keep up with our friends. This is not right, as your friends may be less financially focused than you or have a greater source of income. Trying to keep up with them will see your purse strings tearing apart under the strain.

Remember: your budget is *your* budget, and you should ignore outside voices when planning it. If your boyfriend/girlfriend is leaning too hard on your shoulder and asking for funds you don't have, put them in their place.

This also then perfectly segways into the next pitfall you will face. If you're going to be planning a budget for *your* goals, you might as well also plan it for *your* personality. If you like painting, include whatever expenses may accompany it in your budget. If you enjoy video games, plan for the inevitable need to buy a video game. If you want to go hiking or even drink with your friends every second weekend, put it in the budget. It is all too common for people to think: *Oh no, I'm an adult now. I won't be spending a penny on fun things because it's a waste of money and I'd rather be saving for something more 'adult.'* This way of thinking is utter nonsense. You need to plan for your lifestyle or else you simply won't adhere to your budget. If you like skateboarding and often find yourself hanging out with friends at a diner nearby your usual hangout zones, take some time to plan for this. If you like wearing expensive makeup or consider it a "must" to pay a weekly magazine subscription, then account for this.

For our next budgeting mistake, let us consider the reality that you are incapable of planning for everything. In fact,

113

the only thing you can be sure of is that one (or several) unexpected expenses will pop up somewhere.

These unexpected expenses take many forms, one of which is the tendency to be, well, foreseeable...if your car is old, you can expect it will break. The same assessment can be made for any object really, including your computer or the "fullness" of your shampoo bottle. If your mom's birthday is due in two months, you can expect to buy her a present. If your calendar shows summer vacation is around the corner (or when you get older, a national holiday is coming up), then you can expect that you will be paying a social expense like some alcohol or a trip somewhere. Indeed, some of our more unforeseen expenses can be planned for by taking some time to look at a calendar or assessing the "state" of things around you. Don't let surprises sneak up on you. Furthermore, you can honestly and truly expect something unforeseen to happen. This is an inevitable fact of life. Heck, you might just wake up one day desperately craving a pizza, or perhaps you receive a call from your best friend who begs you to bail him out...in anticipation of this, I recommend actually budgeting for "chaos." That way, if you find a night out with friends is becoming more expensive than you planned, at least you can keep partying and forget about the bill for a bit. Likewise, if the library sends you a bill for an overdue book, at least it won't ruin your finances. The chaos budget should account for both "fun" things (like partying, video games, and pizza), but also bad things (like bills, repairs, or "accidents"). Any money left over should be pooled into your savings account.

Our next downfall of budgeting lies in not saving for a rainy day. In fact, at all times you should be building a comfortable pillow of savings in your account. This was a lesson COVID-19 taught many people quite harshly…for a lot of people, surviving the virus meant having enough savings to outlast 2 to 3 months of hard lockdown with no income, as well as juggling new expenses. The pandemic seems to have receded, but the lesson has not. You should be passively aiming to have enough money available so that you can survive at least two months of unemployment. This is vital. There is no worse fate than living hand to mouth, as often it means you are one day of bad luck away from homelessness.

Lastly, one of our biggest mistakes is thinking our expenses are set in stone. Quite the contrary: Almost all the expenses you wrote down can be modulated by your actions and behaviors. If you wrote down $100 for gas for your car, this can be easily lessened by carpooling or even walking to the store if it is close enough. Likewise, if your rent is too high, consider finding a new place or negotiating with your landlord. The same can be said for almost all costs, including your cell phone provider to your insurance policy; these costs can often be reduced by putting in the occasional effort to research competitors, negotiate, or downscale. More importantly, earlier I spoke of the importance of budgeting for your lifestyle. Well…if it turns out that your lifestyle is too expensive, consider cutting back a bit. There is no need for you to go shopping or drinking with your friends *every* weekend, nor is there a need for you to have a subscription to Netflix, Amazon Prime, Hulu, and HBO. By trimming back on an excessive lifestyle, you'll be able to match your budget far more thoroughly.

Remember: A budget only works if you are willing to stick to it and make some changes to your life. You can't budget like a king when you are paid like a pauper. You can use the budget template provided on the next page to get you started, however, I'd imagine you will be customizing and changing it as you go about learning your own spending patterns.

## Budget Template

| | Fixed Costs: | Fluctuating Costs (Anticipated): | Fluctuating Costs (Actual): | Income: |
|---|---|---|---|---|
| Examples: | Rent, Insurance, Medical, etc. | Anticipated costs of things like: Phone bill, utility, food, etc. | Actual costs of items listed in the preceding column. | All the sources of income available to you. |
| | | | | |
| Total: | | | | |

Income: − Fixed Costs: − Fluctuating Costs (Actual): = Savings:

Total:

\*\*\*

Next, we need to talk about getting a job. Yes, you will be needing one. After all, no amount of budgeting will ever save you if you have nothing to budget with. The fact is, you need to find one way or another to get some money in your bank account each and every month for the rest of your life. Most importantly, you want to do it in a way that you can either enjoy, or at the very least tolerate.

That last bit is vital. It's better to be a happy bus driver than a miserable accountant. This does not mean you should kick back and relax if you are a bus driver, it simply means that it is incredibly important to account for your own personality when you go about finding a decent job. The reasoning for this may also go beyond human happiness, it is a matter of productivity. If you are happy with your work you will do better in it, which will boost your reputation, and in turn, lead to a bountiful harvest of opportunities later in life. The best way to know which kind of jobs you'll excel at is by having taken part in a few jobs before anyways. If you are a creative who likes spending hours reading fantasy novels and fantasizing about all sorts of "scenarios" in your head, perhaps consider becoming a corporate writer (yes, that exists. Who do you think writes the Marvel movies?), or even writing a few books of your own. If you are a creative who has a flair for the more "technical" aspects of things, then perhaps graphic design, 3D animation, or video game development might suit you best. Yet you need not limit your definition of what it means to be a creative; for example, creative thinkers can make potent businesspeople or even investigators.

Likewise, if your thinking is more of a "technical" one, then perhaps going more into IT, accounting, etc., can represent a wise move. However, the personality traits you should consider can become more nuanced. Will you be able to work a 9 to 5 desk job? Given the trends of your generation, the answer probably was an immediate no. But what if I told you that a 9 to 5 desk job, sometimes, involves a lot more walking around and planning, collaborating, or networking? Perhaps that would be more your speed? Of course, some people prefer a good excel spreadsheet, because it carries an air of predictability to it; they would find reassurance in knowing "If I focus, I'll be done by 2," as it allows them to plan a freer day.

I'd recommend going back to the chapter that focuses on archetyping and adapting it to ask the pivotal question: What is my ideal job? What personality traits do I have that I can rely on to make some money? Can I work for someone else? Should I seek to start my own business or open a restaurant? Asking such questions are vital as choosing a good career path can be hard and often necessitates a large commitment from you.

For the most part, when you are young and in your first "stage" of life, I'd recommend focusing on experiencing a broad range of career types first. This may be harder to do if you are studying, however, never underestimate the value of a good internship or part-time job. Some people even "shadow" people for the sake of learning what their career is like, certain charity volunteer positions will often also put you in the thick of things. These are all things you can quickly do as a student to help you out before choosing a major. I wouldn't recommend relying on a google search and a few people's Instagram feeds to get an idea of what a career is like. The things you'll find on google are often adverts of a sort — especially google stories on a phone feed — and I can assure you an Instagram or TikTok post showing the "dream life" of a model, "CEO," fitness coach, influencer, or even programmer, is often filled to the brim with overinflation and won't give you *any* clue what the real job is actually like. Rather, getting hands-on experience and being thrown into a frying pan is a must when you are trying to understand how your personality will gel with a job.

Once you know what you want to do, getting the job can be a challenge. The biggest step is getting past a company's "Applicant Tracking System" or "ATS." These are computer programs that large companies use to scan and discard CVs based on keywords detected. It helps these large companies save time and energy when vetting new candidates, but it also tends to throw out perfect candidates simply because they weren't using the right keywords in their CVs. You need to make sure your CV, cover letter, resumé, or job application doesn't get thrown out by a computer program in order to get into some of the larger companies, although be warned smaller companies will also sometimes use an ATS system. There are many guides on google that explain how to get past these programs. For the most part, you need to understand that you will be "customizing" each application you send to suit the needs of a company. The best way to do this is to spend some time researching them, using the same keywords they like to use, and making sure that a computer will notice these keywords.

Speaking of research, this is another important part of job hunting. Researching a company before interacting with them is a fantastic idea, as it will help you stand out a bit during interviews (and on your CV), by seeming more like a good fit than others who go in blind would.

Once all the research is done, go back to your social media accounts and make sure everything is fully trimmed. Almost all companies and businesses do some social media stalking of their applicants to get a good idea of what the applicant is about; if your accounts are flooded with memes and posts about "screwing over big pharma," then I can assure you even a small town pharmacy will think twice before deciding to hire you. The same can be said for any pictures of you doing a lot of drinking and partying. Although there is nothing wrong with a good time, and most companies won't mind the occasional photo of you with a drink in your hand or having a red-flushed set of cheeks on your face; having hundreds of photos of your best friend Steve passed out drunk besides your pool will be received quite poorly by almost all companies. At the very least, they'll conclude you're a poor friend who would rather mock and display Steve's weakest moments to the world, rather than help him to bed and keep his moments of overindulgence private. If these photos mean a lot to you, consider making them private and displaying only some of your more professional photos.

On that note, there is nothing wrong with not having much of a social media presence. For some it may be a red flag, for others, it will pique curiosity. When it comes to the art of job hunting, it would be wise to at least have a properly set up LinkedIn profile, as this will help your potential employer at least find assurance that your CV isn't somehow fake. However, please take plenty of time adequately setting up your LinkedIn to look professional. I'd recommend browsing other people's profiles and noticing what looks nice and what doesn't.

Next, once you have landed the interview, take some time to practice speaking out loud and getting accustomed to hearing your own voice. You should take the time to know you have value and that there are talents you can bring to the table. Many first-time job seekers will panic at this step, as their lack of experience affords them very little confidence in their own abilities. That is okay, even if you are flooded with uncertainty, rather assume that you "can" do it and that your natural talents will somehow emerge as you learn the job. This is what it means to "fake it till you make it," and it is a practice I highly recommend.

It's important to try your best to sound like you believe you can do the job when you're in an interview, even if your answers make no sense. One of the strangest parts of human beings is that we rather tend to listen to people's energy than their actual answers. So when an interviewer is keeping their attention fully focused on you, your actual answers and the logic they contain will only determine 30% of their approval, the remaining 70% will be determined by your self-belief that you can handle whatever responsibilities they throw at you and that the company would benefit from your presence and influence. If you pull this off well, then even if the interviewer concludes you aren't a good fit, they'll at least like you and they *might* even forward your CV to a place they think needs you.

It is important to keep things friendly, especially in a business environment, but we'll focus a lot on this in the next chapter.

For now, once you've mastered all the steps of job hunting. Let's take a moment to consider if the company is a good fit *for you*. You see, something that most people tend to overlook is that companies have a culture. The culture is maintained by the boss as well as the management, and you'll see that if your way of working or thinking doesn't synch with how the company likes to go about doing things, then it won't matter how hard you work, or talented you are, you and the management team will clash like mortal enemies. Take for example the philosophies of "when" to work. Some people feel like it shouldn't matter if you work a nine to five or an eleven to seven, so long as the work gets done. Now, although this logic is sound, very often some management teams will frown on this, especially corporate-trained ones who want things to run in a predictable way. However, sometimes you will find yourself working for people who say they don't care. You can come in at 2 p.m. and work till 2 a.m., so long you get the work done by the deadline.

Sounds like a dream right?

What if "until the work is done" secretly entails a culture of working 14-hour days?

You see. This is why it is important to not only research a company, but also research the management team and the way they go about enforcing policies. Taking some time to study your managers and learn how they think can help you gain an insight into the culture they will be trying to establish, and perhaps more easily impress them during the interview. This is important, as often when you join a company they will be giving you a mold and expecting you to fit into that mold. This is normal and something you should learn to do, however, if the mold is too uncomfortable it will lead to burnout, fighting, and a manager who treats you poorly even if you are actually doing well. Therefore, during the interview don't be afraid to ask some questions back about some of the procedures that the company follows as well as their personal philosophies on certain matters.

# CHAPTER 6

# MANAGING
# YOUR CIRCLE

One of the most difficult things about growing up is your friends: They tend to grow up, too. While this happens, many things can go wrong or right. One of the most tragic and common of all is that friends will "lock" each other up: meaning that they tend to create their own bubbles, where their united views and values are maintained and pushed within the group, often to an individual's detriment. This can be a powerful tool for overcoming hard times, or a mechanism of abuse and cruelty — the line between which is quite narrow and thin.

But we won't be focusing on that, at least for now. Instead, I'd like us to rather focus on the sheer *power* of a good social circle, as their impact can be quite substantial. You see, the quintessential value of a social circle lies in the social proof that is inherent in the act of interacting with someone. To illustrate my point, let me take you through a basic example.

Let's say for instance that during your college years, you decide to do some light charity/community work, and during this time you come to know one of the other volunteers as an acquaintance. This person spends some time chatting with you as you go about your various "charitable" activities, and you wind up building a degree of rapport with the person. The relationship need not balloon beyond that of a professional acquaintance, all that matters is that the other person comes to learn that you're an "okay" person yourself. Going to see you at the charity work should never feel like a chore to them, nor should they leave interactions with you thinking you were "drama."

That's the only catch to this, you need not "wow" them by being hilarious beyond reason, witty, or deeply charming; but no matter what, your interactions should avoid any negative feelings within them. There is, of course, a greater nuance to this; ideally, you should try and impress them if you can, however, this can cause you some anxiety if you care about people "liking" you too much. Let's avoid a scenario where you overexert yourself trying to impress people, yet still, reap the benefits.

And what are the benefits?

Well, let's next imagine you find yourself 10 years later applying for a job at a firm you usually would stand no chance of getting into. You've spent the past few years floating from one job to another in an industry, never truly catching a break and getting to climb the ladder any higher because you always miss the chance when an opportunity for a promotion arises. You find yourself going to this interview hoping they'll give you a shot at a position with greater pay and responsibilities, yet you inwardly feel that the interview didn't go well, and the interviewer gave you an "I don't trust you" kind of look.

As you walk down the corridor to the elevator, your head slung low as you anticipate you missed another shot, the same acquaintance from your charity years notices you walking past their cubicle.

Ten minutes later, in the break room, that past acquaintance of yours is chatting with the boss when out of curiosity they ask, "Who was that you were in a meeting with?"

"Oh, an applicant for the managerial position that just opened up. Their CV looked promising but when we were talking, well, I don't feel too sure now…"

"Why's that?"

"Well, they weren't what I was expecting. I need someone I can trust, whose heart is focused on more than business and money. I need someone who is focused on people's thinking. The person I met today looked too cold for a position like this. "

"Oh, that's unfortunate…they weren't like that back in college."

"You knew them?"

"Yeah, there was a food drive we volunteered with together at the local chapel. They tended to space out sometimes, but they always came across as a deep thinker to me. We actually got along well, and they always dreamed of doing…never mind, I don't want this to influence your thinking, so I'll just take my coffee and leave the hiring decision to you."

Your past acquaintance winks at the boss as they leave the room, not knowing that they just made a *massive* impact on this guy's decision regarding you.

The boss leaves in his car later that day, and in the back of his mind, he can't shake the hunch that there may be the intertwining influence of fate and destiny in meeting you that day. Somewhere in the back of his mind, he finds himself trusting you a bit more. Not knowing that this trust was borne from a past association with an employee he already trusts. Not knowing that the reason he thinks of fate and destiny boils down to the moment he heard you know his employees, forcing him to ponder that the world may be smaller than he initially thought.

Wouldn't you know it, later that day you get a call from him saying he wants to hire you for a probationary few months later that day, citing he found your credentials impressive, even if you don't perfectly suit his needs.

At last, someone gives you a chance to prove yourself. Citing the credentials you worked *so hard* for as the reason for your triumph; The feeling that you earned it drives you to work hard at your new job, impressing the new boss even more. Meeting your old acquaintance also feels like the work of fate and destiny, making you feel even happier in the new firm. Three years down the line you find yourself promoted yet again, being pushed forth by the swell of positivity that was haphazardly generated by an instant of coincidence.

All this is borne from the aspect of social proofing. What it is, is a simple thing, yet is hard to wholly encapsulate in a simple statement.

You see, as human beings we easily often find ourselves hurt and attacked in life. It is common for most people — the leaders of major firms as well — to rather distrust strangers. In fact, distrusting strangers is a matter of evolutionary survival. Much like our inherent social wiring to avoid change in our established behaviors (which have been keeping us alive), so too do we have a mistrust of strangers.

This mistrust of strangers is logical. Why are they strangers in the first place anyway? Why don't the other tribes know them? Were they chased away from their own lands for doing something wrong? Are they running away from danger and bringing it here? Have they come to hurt us? Will they take from us? Are they enemies?

Yet uniquely, this mistrust of strangers is also paradoxically at odds with another evolutionarily wired trait. *cooperation.* As humans, the basis of our power lies in networking and working together to overcome any obstacle. We are strong together, and the playground of evolutionary survival hammered this truth into us repeatedly. A man who hunts a lion alone is doomed, yet for the African *Maasai* tribes of Kenya, it is a vital coming-of-age tradition when the pubescent boys of a village band together to brutalize the powerful beast with spears, teamwork, and the guidance of an experienced leader.

So to overcome this paradox of instincts, our brains have a uniquely simple "switch off" button when it comes to strangers. The moment we can make *any* link of association between a stranger and someone else, we stop considering them strangers. We will make a judgment of someone based on the company they *used* to keep, no matter how marginal, as it allows us to consider them more than an unknown stranger and rather attributes to them the values of a "group" or "people" that can be later refined depending on the rapport we build later. In the above example, the employer began to associate you with the values he saw in your past acquaintance, a person he knows and works with. Perhaps even he associated you with the values of the chapel that housed the charity event.

This is why ivy league colleges tend to keep producing "high earners". When graduates leave these colleges. The skills or "smart" they have become irrelevant to any prospective employers, who will look at them across the interview table and associate a "Harvard genius" with the spaced-out-looking weirdo sitting there. The boss may not even like the guy, but will give him the benefit of a doubt on association alone anyway, ultimately landing him a high-paying job.

It is also the reason why people in the old days introduced themselves "with" an association. In ancient Japan, it would be best to introduce yourself to a group of unknown (and potentially hostile) villagers as: "I am Taiji, of the Minamoto clan." Rather than: "Taiji, the vagabond." The same logic applies to any medieval movie where peasants introduce themselves as: "Mirelda, daughter of the blacksmith" to the local lord, earning her a semblance of reason to be treated well. A similar phenomenon can also be said for ancient African tribes, who would say they are descendants of Zulu, Maasai, Xhosa, or Venda tribes. The act of doing so establishes the significance of respective values when interacting with other tribes, as people will know "the Zulu's are like this", or "the Venda are from there, thus they like these things" A line of thinking that has led to much suffering in the past, yet at the very least removes the notion that you are a "stranger" and allows people to interact with a semblance of trust and rapport without even knowing each other.

It's a shortcut that, undoubtedly, is the reason for much of mankind's folly and human suffering, yet in the end, it was a vital survival mechanism that has allowed us to make friends quickly when evolution would drive us to stay away from each other. Indeed, the root source of our ignorance simultaneously acts as the ignitor by which we would allow a stranger into our world, establish larger and larger societies, and thereby perpetuate the creation of civilization.

It is therefore to your best advantage to seize this phenomenon to your benefit. You need not obsess over the finer details of getting people to like you; what you should do, however, is learn to become more mindful of who your friends are and what "bubble" you are occupying.

Please do not underestimate the potency of the bubble you occupy. It influences all aspects of your life, your thinking, and your reasoning, your opportunities. In fact, it can go beyond your individual human experience. The influence of social "bubbles" impacts almost everything from consumer spending habits, social hierarchies, society, and political movements. It's a very hard thing to describe, but have you ever wondered how *different* your world would be, had different people surrounded you? They would have exposed you to new social circles, taught you new ways of thinking, and inspired different hobbies.

It is no exaggeration to say that your personality is strongly shaped by the three or four people you spend most of your time with.

This phenomenon is compounded by social media. Heed my warning, you *will*, as a rule, become more like the people who you follow on TikTok, Instagram, etc. The process behind this is an insidious one, yet we see it happen over and over.

Impressionable people find a community online that makes them feel "welcome," and because of this, they find a sense of self there. They will follow people and think, *Oh, yes. I agree with this* or *Oh, yes, I've experienced and felt that before, also*, and they will mistake the ability to emphasize and associate as proof that "I am like this. I should behave like this." Sadly, this leads to much of the craziness we've seen birthed from the internet over the past decade.

The core issue is that people go here desperately in search of that which makes them unique — yet as humans, we are actually so similar and we wish to fit in somewhere; they end up associating with all sorts of ideologies and complex personas, they perhaps even take a step too far and self-diagnose themselves with various mental health illnesses and falsehoods.

As an example, we can look at Dissociative Identity Disorder (DID), a form of mental illness where a person has multiple personalities trapped inside them. Due to TikTok, psychologists have seen an explosion of people entering their clinics with supposed DID. Uniquely, DID is one of the rarest mental health illnesses in the world—with less than 100 cases having been recorded in all of history prior to 1990, and considered to affect no more than 1.5% of the global population (Giedinghagen, 2022). There are entire psychiatric hospitals that have never had a DID case in them.

Yet, mental health practitioners have seen a surge of people below the age of 25 knocking on their doors *insisting* they have DID because they could see they share symptoms with others on TikTok. The past few years have seen an explosion of cases where people are convincing themselves they are developing this hyper-rare disorder *en masse*, and even displaying many of the symptoms. More uniquely, some psychologists have even noticed that these acts of "self-convincing" have led to the manifestation of many severe, and very real, symptoms.

Tragically, these people turn on their social media and find a flood of supportive messages, as well as a strong—vocal—community: sharing symptoms, displaying symptoms, and ultimately, goading symptoms. There have been quite a few studies showing that the act of lying about or convincing yourself you have a symptom actually causes and strengthens it, and you can *indeed* convince yourself you have something you do not.

In fact, during the research of this book, I even came across the tale of a man who had a panic attack, and in turn, convinced himself he had schizophrenia. The poor man even started to experience symptoms and heard voices. Only after two years of anguish did he consider seeking help, at which point he was told he had something else and realized his error; then, 10 years later after realizing he was always just a normal guy who believed a lie; his symptoms were gone — barring the occasional panic attack. His story was chronicled in *The Guardian* in 2007, under the title: "I convinced myself I was going mad" (Rowland, 2007).

The magic bullet?

Realizing he gets to choose who he wants to be. It helped that he surrounded himself with psychologists who could guide him, and real mental health sufferers who he could tell had it far worse.

This is the power of the bubble. Who you surround yourself with determines your truth, especially when you choose to accept or reject it.

The lesson we learn from all this is a simple one. You will become who you surround yourself with. Look at your friends. What are they like? Truth is, you will eventually be like them. At the very least, you'll try to fake it and become like them, until one day you are. If you are lucky, you'll feel you don't fit in and find people who make you feel welcome. We all do this. We all see someone, or a group of people, and say: I have a few of these traits, perhaps I am like them.

The same is valid for your online world. Whoever you follow on your phone, what you watch and fill yourself with, will determine who you become and what you think.

Yet in the end, the truth in the matter is your own choice. You can choose to "report" or flag things as inappropriate for you when a post pops up representing a way of thinking you wish to avoid. With effort, you can train your social media algorithm to show you videos of cats being funny or at least news more useful and practical.

You can take an active choice in determining who you want to be, by looking at others and deciding if these are your people. Yet even then, an onus exists for you to still draw lines between your own beliefs and your friends' beliefs: a need to acknowledge that although you may be deeply similar to some or many people, you don't have to be 100% on the same page as them.

This is the true mark of an adult. It is displayed in the ability to say no in a way that shows certainty and is non-threatening to both the speaker and the listener, and it is experienced as a certainty of who you are, and who you want to be—as well as a pride in where you are trying to go.

*** 

Having said all that, we need to navigate the dark truth that not all friends—even best friends—are good friends. Nor are all bubbles and associations good bubbles and associations. This may seem obvious; it doesn't take much brainpower to realize there are certain groups of people—like Nazis—who you should avoid all association with. Yet, the nature of this truth can often be far sneakier and more insidious. You may not realize what the group of friends you hang out with are like until you look back and see in hindsight what kind of people you were. You could easily have been the school bullies without noticing. Perhaps even, you are victimized by your friends without noticing. It happens far easier than you would imagine.

We can start by discussing the term "toxicity" being thrown around a lot nowadays. Sadly, it is often attributed to whiny pink-haired people on the internet who attack anyone who doesn't think like them with vitriolic ferocity and delusional certainty. In truth, they derive this term from the very astute notion that people can indeed be quite "toxic" toward others, in the sense that a series of subtle behaviors — with time — will break down your character or push you to do things you don't want to. In essence, it is entirely possible and common for two people to be in association in a way where one of you often will take hits to "prop up" the other, often creating a somewhat parasitic association. This is a form of abuse, and it can be quite insidious. The most common you will experience, especially as a young person, is one where you will be "dragged down" to behave in ways you wish to avoid. If your friend smokes, he/she will want you to smoke too so they'll feel less lonely and feel more socially "acceptable." Make no mistake, this will not commonly take the form of a scruffy kid telling you to smoke "or you'll be a loser," like a *Simpsons* cartoon.

In fact, what likely will happen is that your childhood best friend will approach you, with a shy blush on their face, wanting to share a secret. Upon much prodding and begging it will eventually be revealed that they "tried a cigarette." A few months, weeks, or even years can pass; after some time, and talking, you find yourself sneaking away to a spot for them to smoke in order to accommodate their newfound hobby — without necessarily partaking yourself, you'll just be there to keep them company. Eventually, out of curiosity, you'll ask to try one yourself. The aforementioned friend will likely appreciate the moment to connect and share an experience, and you'll likely find a positive interaction occurs during this first cigarette. Because of this, your slow descent into doing something you strongly claimed you would "never do" has begun — fueled by the very human need for connection and reciprocation. The same narrative applies to anything and everything from alcohol, to drugs, to certain social behaviors, cults, or even political movements. People seldom do things when threatened, but they will try things if their friends show that it can be "normal," as a need will form to be a "part" of it.

Now, how bad all this is, is a matter of debate. Obviously, drugs and smoking are bad. Yet the truth is the world won't end if you and your best friend had a smoking phase during your early 20s. The fact is, you'll likely laugh about it one day when you are 50 and entertain each other with memories of hiding on the roof to avoid getting caught.

The issue, however, lies not then in being "dragged down," but rather in being "kept" there. For example: Imagine saying you want to quit smoking, only to hear that you're being "a chicken"; perhaps your friends spend the next hour teasing you, smoking in front of you, insisting that the cigarettes are great and you're missing out. Chances are good you'll join in. Heck, even if they do no such thing, you'll likely join them anyway if they seem awkward and uncertain about you *not* smoking when they are smoking.

The danger is, that the same mentality can apply to drugs and binge drinking, or unwanted social concepts like racism or elitism. Even for many adults, saying no to a drink can be hard in a social setting—especially when everyone else gives them a look that says, "Buzzkill!"

Now, I'm not advocating that you be a buzzkill, what I want to do however is draw your attention to the reality that some groups of people will sometimes validate or invalidate your behavior depending on how it makes them feel *about themselves*. Very often, people taking the time to mess with you, tease you, mock you, or react negatively to you are often saying more about themselves than about you. If someone gets upset with you for not drinking with them or tries hard to convince you to join, chances are it simply means they aren't comfortable drinking alone.

This is a core truth about human psychology that very few people learn, yet most functional adults have come to grasp it in one way or another. Usually when someone has a fixation or a problem with you, it's actually a lot more about themselves.

Often without either of you noticing.

Once again though, it can be a matter of debate how "insidious" this is. After all, no one wants to drink alone, so what is wrong with wanting to convince someone to join you? Well...again, we can draw the line further by looking at the core interactions at play.

Remember, this whole conversation on toxicity started out by stating the behaviors we see are "parasitic." Because at some point, a friendly attempt to make you have a drink *can* transition into an attempt to make you the drunkest person at the party, and hence the local laughing stock for everyone else. Now, the friend who initially wanted you to join for one drink can have his own drinking behavior validated by your drunkenness.

The line between companionship and abuse exists somewhere on the road between these two points, and you must judge for yourself where to draw it.

I cannot tell you where to nail down the line, you'll need to decide for yourself depending on your friends. What I can tell you is this: Toxic friends will make you feel like the fool. You'll be something to point at and laugh about from time to time, and they may ask you to laugh and joke about things you don't want to laugh about thereafter. They'll make you feel pressured to behave in certain ways and they'll get upset when you don't, or try to goad and encourage certain behavior from you. They can also be very charismatic as they go about doing this. You often won't notice until you get put in a situation you are entirely unhappy with.

This is all very subconscious, of course; no one wakes up thinking, *I want to be abusive today.* Instead, what happens is a matter of subtle cause and effect within their hearts. They'll feel good about themselves when they put you in certain situations, and they'll go about pursuing this good feeling passively without noticing they do it; much like how you'll go to the kitchen when you feel hungry, even though you have no plan on what to do when you get there.

The obvious solution is to draw their attention to this. If they truly are your friends, they'll respect what you told them about their behavior and try to stop. Yet at this point we can see our second red flag: Perhaps they don't care or don't respect what you told them. If this happens it may hurt, but don't be fooled into thinking you're at fault, or not worth being respected, or undeserving of being bullied. You're just trapped in a toxic bubble at this point with people who give you negative feedback for the things you'll do. They won't respect your feelings, they won't honor your wishes, and they won't be good friends. At this point, your best move is to realize the issue is with them and move on.

It's best to do this as soon as possible. You see, chances are good this form of toxic abuse transitions into personalities and interests. You may have an interest in poetry, painting, or calculus that your friends think is *very* lame, and they'll often mock you or point out your "weirdness" whenever you mention these interests. This is highly toxic behavior and a sign of deep inner jealousy. They may even work together to maintain the status quo and openly tell you they think your interest in art or calculus is meaningless as a group. They may also judge your desire to rather spend time with other groups of people. This happens because groups of people form "bubbles," and within these bubbles, certain traits are admirable while others are not. Rather than try to tolerate the abuse of a bubble whose traits you've begun to outgrow, rather slowly cut back ties and seek a bubble where your traits are praised or admired. This can do wonders for your self-development.

It is vital to take the time and notice these potentially negative influences, after all, our long-term goal is to find a niche in a society where we can earn money, feel respected, and enjoy life while simultaneously giving back to our children and our communities. It is here where fulfillment lies, and it can be hard to reach for it when the people around us continuously break our dreams, talents, and interests down; compare us, and tell us our interests don't matter. If you allow these influences, you may struggle to motivate yourself. It can be hard to explore your talents when a voice nags you in the back of your head that it will lead nowhere, or that you will fail, and your friends will mock you.

Tragically, these influences can come from adult sources, also...our parents, uncles and aunts, teachers, or even grandparents can openly mock our behavior, beliefs, values, talents, or way of thinking at family gatherings, often saying afterward that they are trying to teach us something, protect us from something, or denying that they did it. In these cases, find ways to get away or shut out that influence. The truth is, many of the adults around you are actually quite broken people, and it can easily happen that such a broken person is raising you. You cannot change this about them, but you can decide for yourself if you'll listen or internalize what they say. Just learn to ignore them until you can get away from them, and reach out to people you think may be sympathetic to your plights.

You cannot control the world around you, but you can control the world within.

Of course, we should also be hesitant to judge these negative influences and toxic bubbles as being fueled by intentional malevolence, accidental cause-and-effect, or the result of a hard and broken life, as they need not be as dire.

Indeed, all this talk of "toxicity," "abuse," or "parasitism" can easily fuel internal feelings of betrayal and anger toward people around you who may not deserve it, especially if they tend to shut down the things you say or disapprove of the things you believe. Often, however, these things need not be taken to such a high level of antagonism or as proof of greater darkness or malintent afoot.

All people on earth will experience a state of disagreement with their current bubble at one point or another in their lives, and the source of this is seldom an act of dire maliciousness. In fact, it is often a symptom of growing apart.

As I mentioned, social circles and groups of people maintain their own culture and belief system, often these "mini-cultures" exist within families, between different groups of friends, or in places of work and worship. So what happens if you grow up in this "mini-culture" and eventually begin to reach beyond it? Well…often you'll receive the ire of those who feel most comfortable in their self-made world, as you are now beginning to walk down "the wrong path." They may also fear losing you and seek to hold you back subconsciously.

Remember, humans are social creatures, and we will often take subconscious steps to keep the group big and happy.

This is often why we tend to see people act out and get into strained arguments with their parents during their teen years. Very often when you transition into puberty, your mind will begin to develop to a point where it desires to discover and express its own values. It is as common as sunshine for parents to react to this quite badly, as the values may be quite different from the ones they are trying to instill. You may express interest in things that they find no value in. This battle of ideologies will happen again many times in your life, your first may be with your parents as a teenager, yet your second will likely be with your childhood friends who you outgrow later in life, followed by further growth spurts during your late 20s and again when you have kids of your own, and again when those kids become teenagers themselves...

It is important to make peace with the fact that you'll need to learn to get along with people who refuse to think along your lines or approve of your reasoning of thought. Most importantly, you need to come to terms with the fact that just because some groups of people may endeavor to break down your inner world, doesn't mean they are "right" or that you should heed their opinion, nor does it mean they are evil, and they must be resisted at all costs.

What should be done is for you to take a moment to realize they are reflective of *them* and not *you,* and as such, you can take a moment to listen and decide later if you want to follow.

When all is said and done, rather decide for yourself "who you are" and maintain this world within as you chose to ignore unwanted outside forces and find more supportive voices. This task can easily be a lifelong journey, but it is undoubtedly a worthwhile one.

\*\*\*

So what makes it so worthwhile? Well, the same series of negative outcomes we see born from an abusive or toxic circle can easily be replaced by a series of positive outcomes when we find a circle that lets us grow and is supportive of our goals in life.

One of the greatest gifts you can give yourself is a social circle where you feel welcome, accepted, and supported. A wholesome little bubble of friends to resist the world with.

Much like how a negative group can break us down and keep us there, so too can a positive one lift us up beyond ourselves and raise us high. You see, although you do have a choice in how you will go about digesting external voices and choosing for yourself if you want to internalize someone else's words, life becomes much easier when you never even need to take the time to digest and judge someone else's words. A positive voice that encourages you swallows easily and feeds you well when you internalize it. Always take the time to listen to someone's praise; even if you think they're just saying something nice for the sake of being "polite," they're still technically showing an attempt to uplift you, which is worth its weight in gold and can often help you stay motivated when your mind wants to make it easier to give up. Even the consistent kind words of one person can sustain your self-belief for years. Of course, there is a separate risk of surrounding yourself with "yes men", but rather be a happy fool than an abused victim, your life prospects will be better.

Of course, there are benefits to a good social sphere beyond simply a positive voice to keep you motivated. The first and most important is the chance of having a "team." This may not sound like much, but a group of friends trying to pursue a business is the key primary ingredient to starting any business or endeavor. Indeed, having a team is a powerful force that can open up many doors for you.

Very often, when starting out a business; a lot of work will need to be done, after hours, for little to no pay. When businesses start they are often an act of love that is pursued by a group of friends who are collectively chasing a shared dream. Look at Facebook, this multi-billion dollar company started as a small dorm room social experiment between a group of three friends, all of whom worked for free using their spare time in-between studies. In fact, almost all companies start off this way.

Even in my own case, I and my friends pursued a shared dream of owning a record label. We each had talents we could contribute in different ways to get the job done. Without my team, that venture would never have had a chance of going forward. If you'll recall me saying earlier, we had to work overtime outside of work, investing our own money and free time in order to produce quality releases with our artists and network with radio stations and various clubs. All of this was sustained with friendship and passion as the sole source of funding, and it faded when those passions shifted elsewhere, and we had to start focusing on other priorities in our life.

My advice here is not that you should go out and make friends for the sake of using them as free labor, nor should you try and convince your friends to work for you for free by leaning on their shoulders…instead, what I am trying to say is that if you can find a group of people who are interested in the same things that you are, then you will find yourselves forming a cohesive team by human instinct alone, and ultimately organically pursuing dreams together in an attempt to make your lives fulfilling, as humans tend to do. This has been the birthplace of most of the institutions you see around you, with passionate people networking and building things. This is how most universities, sports teams, record labels, companies, and to some extent nations are born. Toward this end, the best thing you can give yourself is doing the things you want to do, meeting the people who are interested in the same things as you, exploring those passions together, and allowing whatever should develop to develop organically.

On that note, we need to talk about networking. As I mentioned above, social proofing is a mechanism human beings use to judge if a person can be "worked with" or trusted, this is an aspect of life you'll need to make peace with. You're going to have an incredibly tough time building a career if you don't bother talking or attending social events for your office. Networking is an incredibly powerful tool that can open a broad range of doors for you in your professional life.

The most obvious godsend it will give you is by helping you advance your career and landing you a good job, and this is no small matter. Most people do not earn their jobs in a "literal" way (i.e., work hard for 2 years and get a promotion), instead, they make friends with the right people and have their names mentioned during key conversations at meetings. In fact, some studies seem to indicate that up to 80% of positions are filled through networking and professional contact (Cole, 2019). In other words, most people get a job by being known by the right people; or being offered one by someone who knows them. Although preparing for an interview and squeezing your way into a company is always an option, often, taking the time to talk to people at the neighborhood barbeque can often open doors you wouldn't expect.

Yet there are additional advantages to networking you would never consider. The most profound of which is through the cultivation and generation of ideas.

Remember when we talked about how the key human superpower is communication? It is a factor that sets us apart and elevates us above the normalcy of other animals, by allowing us to speak possibilities and have them merge with other possibilities, inevitably advancing civilization. You will notice that the most powerful and effective teams, those who produce the greatest works, achieve this by collaboration and sharing ideas that are aimed at a shared vision.

This is why networking with others who have the same passions as you is so important, as in doing so you are not only exposing yourself to potential job advances, but you are more vitally exposing yourself to their inner credo and their tenets of life.

If you are for example a programmer, few things will make you as powerful as the ability to discuss code with other programmers. In doing so you will be exposed to their patterns, their way of doing things, their shortcuts; and most vitally: you will learn from them the essence of how they think. If you have an ounce of wisdom you will look at what others are doing, realize why it is smarter than what you are doing, and seek to incorporate it. When you do this, it won't matter what career or industry you follow, you will always become the most competent person in the room.

The world is a complex place, there are many things happening that are not ever fully explained in any one book; ideas and philosophies floating about that you may never have considered possible or useful. Yet when you keep your ears open and expose yourself to them, you will see your own thinking and personal credo toward your work refined to a point where others will want to listen to you.

And lastly, when we take the time to network, we are indirectly building our confidence. Let's say for instance the manager at your office is always breaking you down, or your buddy at college is always telling you your studies won't matter. This force will inevitably lead you to think it is true.

You could walk around for months, even years, thinking that your work is subpar or worthless. Until the day comes that you happen to talk to a manager from another office, a peer, or you meet a new person in class...and they can't help but point out how brilliant your ideas are, or how unique they find your way of looking at things. Suddenly, the possibility may be introduced into your world that you may *actually* be doing something right.

This example may be a bit gruffer than the actual truth of how things will play down, as often what will happen will be far more subtle and lodged in the ethos of a conversation. Indeed, you will be talking to new people and feeling something "good" within yourself without fully being able to specify why. This good feeling is in essence your deeper subconscious noticing that people are treating you like you have value, like how the other person in the conversation looked at you with admiration or curiosity. and cementing the idea within you that you actually have an idea of what you're talking about.

With time, this inner belief can manifest into a force that would be capable of displaying your higher value to the world. Of course, you can cultivate this by learning to talk to yourself well, but a nice shortcut can be found simply in taking the time to talk to others and gather their opinions on things. There are many ideas, opinions, and philosophies out there, each is a puzzle piece that could slot perfectly into your own personal core of living and lead to a more well-rounded, confident, and professional version of yourself. Therefore, the act of networking not only expands your career options and makes you a more capable thinker, but it actually boosts your confidence as a domino effect begins to occur and you keep meeting new people at a faster pace.

\*\*\*

Now, I'd like to take you into the details and the nitty-gritty of how you should go about expanding your circle.

To start, the most dangerous mistake you can make is approaching people for their "usefulness."

All people have an inner radar for when someone wants something we have, this is the reason your gut instinct is to ignore the beggar outside a gas station store, when in truth it would be morally superior to treat the beggar well and buy them a treat. Yet regardless of the correct moral path, you'll do everything in your power to avoid eye contact and reject the beggar, fueled by your own inner instinct to avoid people who "want" something from you.

The same principle is at play in a reverse situation. If you go to a social event at work, and immediately walk up to the boss for the sake of trying to chat him/her up, everyone will notice; and although they may react politely, the interaction won't be sincere, and they'll be quite aware that you just want to use them. In the worst case, people will outright reject you and make fun of you later for doing this.

If you want something from someone; be direct about it, and don't be desperate about it. Don't kiss your boss' butt cheeks in the hope of a raise or promotion, walk up to them and say: "I'd like the promotion" in a manner that doesn't sound like begging. If you can maintain the aura that your world won't end if they say no, then you won't come across as desperate.

Rather be more excited about the fact you were brave enough to ask than afraid if they say no; this will come across well, and even if they say no the confidence you oozed will make them think of you next time a promotion is discussed. They may even like your attitude and invite you to hang out informally, opening new doors.

But most important of all, is to rather let your social choices be guided more by your curiosity and need to have fun than a need to gain something. Your interest and opinions primarily are what should guide the interactions you seek to build, with possible benefits being only a secondary — background — factor. This way, the energy you exude will be more authentic and grounded in "who you are," rather than coming across as a desperate schmoozer.

The act of trying to make friends and talking to the people around you ultimately opens the doors to people's hearts, so you don't need to do more than say "Hi" and talk about what interests you, and ask people what interests them. This is actually a very intuitive mechanism, as you must remember, you literally have *millions* of ancestors who *all* had to be social in order to survive. This means that you should have more than enough instinct to guide your way through any social situation and generate a rapport — aka the story between people.

If you wish to build a network, start talking to someone — anyone — that in some way shares some of your interests, as ultimately, they can connect you to the group that you wish to be a part of; in this way, you'll quickly notice your social circle adapting and expanding organically as you meet people who you like or dislike. Often, in the beginning, people may be slightly cautious as they get to know you and can scare off quickly, but simply by being honest, present, and patient; you'll find they'll slowly open up and a rapport will form between you and the people you wish to know.

Now, this is where things get interesting. You see, due to the rule of "social proofing" I discussed earlier, the act of being seen socializing with some people actually will make it easier for those who are seeing you to trust you. To put it this way, if someone sees you walking down a hallway and talking to someone, rather than walking alone, they'll be a lot more willing to chat with you themselves. Bonus points if they happen to know the person somewhat. Extra bonus points if they know the person you're talking to well.

Please, do not spend your time obsessing over "being seen" talking to people, or the "right" people. This is a path to a lot of narcissism, elitism, and suffering; and people will notice you're using them. The only point I want to get across is that networking can easily have a wonderful snowball effect that you can ride, so long as you simply let curiosity, the joy of connection, and a need to share your ideas guide the interaction.

Never ask yourself what people can do for you, instead focus only on what you can do for people.

This could be anything: Your opinions, your ideas, your humor, your intellect, your sympathy, a patient ear, whatever you can attribute value to. Offer this to the people freely and seek to enjoy spending time with them, whatever benefits they can offer you will be revealed organically with time as they learn to trust you. Connecting with others is mostly an act of realizing you have something interesting to say and saying it; or at least it starts with the realization that the things you want to say *are* interesting, and thus you should feel good about giving it to someone.

As a secondary tip, try to seek a diversification of your circles. If you are trying to make an app that can transpose the noises an instrument makes into sheet music that can be read by others, then not only would it be worth your time to talk to a few programmers, but perhaps also musicians, music teachers, mathematicians, sound engineers, etc. There may be a long list of people that can contribute to your project and who may be interested in your idea, or at least talking to you about the idea (perhaps intellectual property lawyers may also have a few opinions to share...). Therefore, never limit yourself to a "type" of person; always practice your ability to connect with a broad host of characters.

This counts not only for professions and interests but age groups as well. A 40-year-old musician may have different insights than a 20-year-old musician, so don't be afraid to talk to the older crowd as if you are equal, because the truth is you kind of already are. The older you get the less age matters. It is said that by 25 the brain has fully developed, and I'd reckon you add 2 years to get things settled. This means that by the time you're 26 or 27, you're on par with any 40 or 50-year-old, meaning you should talk to them freely. If you're younger than that, never forget that the brain is *mostly* developed by the time you turn 20, so you've very much got the correct idea assuming that you can talk to a 50-year-old like an equal, just be aware you can still learn a thing or two from the older folks as you go about "fitting in."

# CHAPTER 7

# MAKE YOUR MONEY MATTER

S o the first thing you'll realize when you start getting some money in your life and earning a paycheck is that you hate taxes.

This feeling is normal and an inevitable fate for all who enter adulthood. Not only is it upsetting to see a gross difference between the check promised to you each month and the *actual* money you get to keep, but the whole process of reporting your income, calculating how much tax you should pay, and figuring out which tax breaks apply to you can be a bit daunting. Therefore, the first initial gut feeling most will have is to want to "avoid" the whole mess. Of course, this is so evidently the wrong choice that it's a decision most will never make.

To start, it's illegal.

It's very illegal — and traceable.

This means that you will probably be caught if you attempt tax evasion; and if you are caught attempting tax evasion, then jail time is a *very* real possibility, a possibility that should scare you senseless — as it does most others. To add to the danger, your finances are traced and monitored through your bank account, by a computer. This means that *if* you have a bank account, then the money in that account is likely monitored by a computer that does a series of calculations to monitor how much you *probably* earn, and how you probably spend it, making the act of tax evasion near impossible to get away with. Even the slyest and most infamous of criminals often find themselves caught in the traps set by their own bank accounts. Even the powerful mafia kingpins of the 1950s, including Al Capone, were brought to their knees by their failure to respect an accountant's ability to notice they have more money than they should.

Of course, if the amount you didn't pay is relatively small and you can in some way argue you didn't know, you will probably be left with a slap on the hand in the form of a fine as well as being kept under the microscope for a while. That being said, you still want to avoid all this at all costs, as the whole affair of being audited and appearing in a court will be so exhausting and scary that in truth; it would simply have been easier to pay your taxes...especially once you see how big those fines can get.

It is because of the danger of *not* paying taxes, that most people inevitably decide to pay their taxes. Of course, I'd argue that this way of thinking is in no way positive at all.

Taxes are the oil that keeps the gears turning. Whenever you turn on a light in your home, walk in the streets, look at a fountain in a park, hear about a successful police drug bust on the news, see a fighter jet roar over your head, or see a kid get a govt scholarship; then those are the miracles of tax. Taxes, for better or worse, are what can make your country — and your community — worth living in. To that end, the act of paying taxes is an act of generosity and a moment you can feel proud of. It is a way to contribute to the world around you, and a pledge of support for your fellow man.

Sure, you cannot control how the tax dollars are spent and you may find yourself disagreeing a lot with where most of it is being sent, but if the central tax pool is large enough then whatever is left over after being used "wrongly" can *still* do an incredible amount of good. This means that even in a world where you feel each and every dollar is used unwisely, it still becomes worth it to pay your taxes. This is because if the government finds itself short on funds, then it may be forced to make even more risky calls based on a stringent priority list, yet this list becomes far broader and more forgiving if you can help keep the coffers full.

To that end; please pay your tax, even if the amount paid is minuscule, it is a civic duty to do so and when everyone does it, your country is empowered to reach for more and can become a better place to live. It very much is the most direct way to know you are contributing to the world and contributing to your community.

As a final note, just because you pay a policeman's salary or a park ranger's salary through tax, does not mean they work *for* you. In truth, they work for the government, and it is the government instead that is *supposed* to account for your well being as it spends the communities' money (not your money). In other words, if you disagree with a civil servant's approach to you or the rules they enforce, take it up with the government, not the person trying to handcuff you. Paying taxes does not mean you are entitled to anything, it simply means you are contributing to your society; not the owner of it.

In America, the tax year ends on April 15. This means that you need to "do your taxes" before April 15 each year. This is what is meant when you hear people talk about the "financial year," as all major companies, banks, stock brokers, lawyers, investors, bakers, teachers, Instagrammers, TikTokers, writers, comedians, and small businesses must have their finances in order by this date and submitted to the most accurate degree possible. Much of the financial world will swing on this pendulum, as most hiring or firing will be done in consequence to this date, as well as most major financial decisions such as firm takeovers, shareholder meetings, charity contributions, property purchases, medical scheme announcements, etc. Therefore, it is in your best interest to have this date in mind when interacting with the world. If a firm would get a tax break for hiring you (perhaps you have a disability), then your chances of getting hired may increase near this date. Likewise, since capital gains have different tax rules, many people tend to make property purchases before the 15 of April in order to lessen their tax load.

For those who don't know, capital gains tax refers to the taxes applied to anything you own which can be defined as "capital." Hence, it refers to things that contribute to your "theoretical" wealth, or can earn you money passively. Thus, things like stocks, property, business ownership, bonds, furniture, a collection of wines, and even car ownership all count as capital, as you can theoretically trade them for value and use them to "store" money, and potentially earn money based on the prices you trade them at. In other words, capital refers to any asset that you own that has value and you can trade or use to make money. As mentioned, when you make/lose money by buying or selling cars, bonds, stocks, or property, then a unique tax applies called "capital gains tax," which is often lower than normal tax (although this depends on what you already own, and how much you earn). For the most part, if you own or sell such things I'd recommend doing some research on capital gains tax surrounding the asset in question.

But let's not get ahead of ourselves.

To start, an in-depth discussion on taxes is far beyond the scope of this book for many reasons.

You see, the main issue is that tax laws actually change very quickly depending on the year, as well as who is in charge. These changes are luckily not too arbitrary, they often follow the logic of current happenings in the economy and revolve around dictating the percentage to be paid each year. However, the act of discussing them would be irrelevant, as they may change quite a bit by the time this book reaches your hands. Furthermore, they can become incredibly nuanced the more we go down this rabbit hole.

I could easily dedicate several chapters to discussing what is/isn't defined as a capital asset; only for a few of the definitions I used to be changed a year later depending on political movements. court cases, or economical observations made by the Internal Revenue Service (IRS).

This is why you get people who specialize in navigating and understanding the various tax laws and how they apply.

So, instead, I will convey to you the core principles at work and expect that you'll be wise enough to research the topic more in-depth when you want to make tax-based decisions in your life. The IRS also has a downloadable app as well as a series of calculators, information services, and tools on its website designed to make the process as easy as possible. So I recommend you take your tax-based questions there.

To start, the idea is that you will be taxed based on your yearly income, not monthly. Therefore, it does not matter much how many dollars you earn each month, what matters is the amount of money you made for the past year, and that a percentage will be levied onto it. This means that your tax is often calculated based on how much you are *predicted* to make, and many tax laws take account of this and come with an assortment of concessions to overlook your mistakes if you fall short.

Now before you get excited, you need to remember that the system is set up in such a way that you'll be paying as you earn. For most people earning a constant monthly salary, your employer will automatically be taking a cut of your paycheck each month and sending it to the IRS. This deducted amount depends on the current federal tax — which applies to all Americans globally and is determined by the amount you earn; the state tax — which can differ depending on your state, some states don't have any income taxes and some don't levy the tax on your monthly income, so make sure to look up your own state's laws regarding this; and lastly your municipal tax, which depends on the decisions made by your town mayor/counselor and often is used to fund special local initiatives. The good news is that if you have a 9 to 5 job chances are good most of your taxes will be sorted, however, you have a responsibility to ensure that your employer *actually* does this right.

You'd be surprised how often it can happen that a small company or firm won't bother doing their employee's taxes, or doing it wrongly, only for it to cause a disaster down the line for many people. For that reason alone, double-check your contract as well as your monthly paycheck. If your employer does everything well, they should have clearly indicated to you somehow that a cut was sent to the IRS along with some proof. If not, make sure to keep these paychecks somewhere safe so that they can save your bacon when filing your taxes in April. Perhaps consider asking your employer for some proof of their tax payments that you can keep on your end.

Now, we must acknowledge that many people earn their money less consistently than this. Some people run a bed and breakfast or own a comic book store, and their sales can be quite seasonal; or perhaps they make most of their money through sponsorships on social media, which can fluctuate quite dramatically from month to month. Because of this, it is common and strongly recommended by the IRS to file taxes in a quarterly fashion. Meaning an expectation exists for you to pay your taxes four times a year at least, based on your earning projections.

Now, as mentioned earlier, many businesses are seasonal. During the summer, an ice cream truck will make a lot more cash than in the winter. The IRS knows this, and you are expected to declare such seasonality at the time of paying the quarterly taxes, and you are expected to "overpay" during the times when you are flushed with cash. Make sure to carefully investigate which such laws are applicable to you, as a general rule, simply try to pay as you earn.

Your expected earning projections are based on the money you earned last year, so if your ice cream truck made $40,000 in an entire year, this puts you in the second federal earnings bracket at 12%.

12% of $40,000 is $4,800.

Thus, if you made $40,000 last year, then you are expected to pay $4,800 this year no matter what, and you are even permitted to pay most of it during the summer when most of your sales occur. When the end of the tax season arrives on April 15, submit all the taxes you paid, your earnings, as well as proof of payments for deductibles like service costs for the truck, gas for the truck, a laptop for work, the cost of ice cream, bills from business meetings, medical, etc. Don't forget that you also need to pay state and municipal taxes, which differ in amount and applicability depending on your state and municipality.

The IRS will review how much money you made, how much of it was spent to keep the business afloat (the deductibles), and how much taxes you paid each quarter. At this point, if you paid most of it (above 90%), then you will be in "safe harbor," and you'll simply be asked to pay slightly more (or you may not, depending on the nuance of your situation). Likewise, if you overpaid they may give you money back in the form of a "tax return," which can sometimes be a bit more than you paid as a "thank you" in the form of additional interest.

Let's quickly talk about deductibles. These are often the costs you made in order to stay afloat. In the case of the ice cream truck, this means that if you had to replace a tire for the truck, you should include that payment slip from the dealer in your taxes in order to reflect the costs of "staying alive," which the IRS will account for when determining if your taxes are well paid. In essence, the idea is that you should not be taxed if your money was spent on deductibles, so if you made $40,000 in a year with your ice cream truck, but $15,000 of it was spent on keeping the truck functional and the freezer full of ice cream, then you should only be taxed for $25,000, which is significantly less taxes to pay as you pay on a percentage-per-dollar basis. Additionally, capital gains are somewhat considered deductibles as well, so you should add the amount you paid for the truck, in addition to any other capital assets you own, to the deductibles. Usually, the idea is you pay a percentage based on the money you made with the capital asset, so if you bought a home for $400,000 and eventually sell it for $600,000, then you need to pay taxes on the $200,000 earnings you made for the sale. Likewise, the purchase or resale of your ice cream truck could help reduce your tax if you lost a lot of money in the process.

Returning to the example of taxes based on an ice cream truck; if you were taxed for $40,000 from the previous year's sales, you should aim for a target of $4,800 as expected still. Any overpaid tax after accounting for deductibles will be returned to you as a tax return when the tax year ends. However, never put yourself in a situation where you can't pay the bills because of taxes. Remember, the tax system only wants your "extra" money. Make sure to take care of yourself first, be mindful of roughly how much you owe the government second, and try to deal honestly with the IRS regarding your taxes.

That way, the IRS will always account for your income fairly and see that you've been honest. Since tax laws are complex, change often, and people have no idea how they work; the IRS can actually be quite forgiving if it is clear you are trying to be honest with them. If you can't pay taxes because rent and fuel costs are too high, consider moving somewhere cheaper and taking the bus; because in that case, it means you're living above your means. Always stay informed of local tax laws and plan your life accordingly.

The same principles are applicable no matter what you do, so if you are a social media influencer, then your earnings may or may not be seasonal depending on your niche and the sponsorship contracts you've signed. Your deductibles will be things like the costs of your phone, data package, etc. Perhaps even the fuel/travel to go to certain locations or events. Likewise, the amount you are expected to pay depends on the earnings you made last year as an influencer.

That being said, if it is your first year earning a living as an influencer or ice cream seller and you have no past sales record, then you should pay taxes based on your quarterly earnings. The dates to file quarterly taxes are usually set to the 15th of April, June, September, and January, respectively. Meaning that by the 15th of September, you are expected to pay taxes based on the money you made between June the 1st and August the 31st (The previous 3 months excluding September itself). On the 15th of April, the taxes for your whole year are accounted for and any shortfalls or overpayments you accidentally made will be asked for or given back to you.

The last point we can touch on is the manner in which your tax situation will differ depending on the context of your life. You are already aware that the taxes you should pay differ depending on the state you live in, as well as the manner in which you earn money. However, the taxes can also fluctuate depending on your age, your marital status, if you are a widow, if you have a disability, if you have kids, or if you are the "head" of a household (the primary breadwinner.) Furthermore, the differences involved vary depending on your state or municipality. Marital status and age are taxed on a federal level, meaning that the "global" tax applicable to everyone becomes less if you are over 65 years old. Likewise, married couples who share their finances pay different taxes than those who don't across the whole United States.

You see, the reason tax laws become so complex is because, over the years, they were written to accommodate as many different lives as possible, while also serving a broad host of problems and accounting for many factors. This is why the services of a good tax broker are often so sought after and highly recommended when earning and working with large volumes of money. If you are not earning a lot, the good news is that there are many free tax calculators available online, as well as a ton of information on the IRS website. The IRS will assist you freely when filing taxes, so make sure to put in the effort and reach out, and they'll help you out. Furthermore, as mentioned at the start of the chapter, the IRS does have an assortment of electronic forms and tools that can help you, including a downloadable cell phone app called "IRS2Go" which was designed to navigate much of the hassle commonly involved.

Taxes can be complex, but they need to make sure everyone can understand and pay them, so the tools are out there for you to find a way if you try

*** 

Now we can move on to a few other financial responsibilities worth thinking about. Like our above talk on taxes, the rabbit hole can easily run a tad deep, so we are only going to mention a few points worth mentioning. That being said, for the most part, you need to learn to plan your finances in such a way that you have accounted for emergencies and the chaos that life brings, so we are now going to talk about insurance, Social Security, and retirement funding.

Now, we can start by saying that the core principle behind all of this is that you will be investing money for a rainy day. If you are super rich, you'll be better off simply locking a large sum of cash away in a good savings account and only accessing it when your house burns down, this way, you'll save a lot more money than people who pay insurance each month. If you are super poor and cannot afford insurance, saving every penny is the only way forward.

That being said, this advice will help almost none of you. Since very few of you will be so poor that you'll need to save every penny in order to buy a sandwich every second day, and very few of you will be so rich that you can buy a house for $2,000,000 and immediately put another $2,000,000 in a savings account in case things go wrong.

For most of us, financing schemes like insurance, Social Security, medical aid, and retirement funding will be the only hope of ever surviving a bad day.

Sure, you'll get upset at having to put away $100 every month for house insurance that you may never need. In fact, you'll be even more upset after 10 years when you realize you spent $12,000 on "nothing." But you'll thank heaven you have insurance when a tornado, burglary, or fire takes everything from you and the insurance company gives you $200,000 to help you recover. It could be entirely possible for you to pay insurance every month for 30 years, never needing it once, deciding to cancel it, and 2 months later the house burns down.

It's terrifying but it is very possible and has happened more times in history than you'd like to hear.

So, let's cover the basics.

To start, as an individual, you should strive to make sure you have medical aid first and foremost. This is an area of personal financing you should not hold back on and fulfill to the best of your ability, and should be placed high on your priority list. Medical aid can be quite expensive — especially in America — but is an absolute must, *especially* in America, where medical care is significantly more expensive than anywhere else in the world. Nothing will break your heart more than being unable to afford a vital surgery simply because you'd rather have saved $20 a month, or not being able to receive the therapy you need to walk straight because your insurance won't cover it.

There are more than enough horror stories of people refusing an ambulance because of the financial repercussions, as well as being diverted to hospitals further away because insurance won't cover the care at the "closest" hospitals. To that end, read your insurance package's policies meticulously and try to avoid any policies that state you are only covered by "certain" practitioners or limit specialist care to "twice per year." Preferably, you'd want an insurance package that will let you see whatever doctor you want, at whatever hospital you want. Furthermore, in the event of an emergency, you'll probably end up seeing three to four specialists at least three to five times each *in a few days*. So make sure your insurance will go that far or at least has a clause that accounts for emergency care regarding specialists. Lastly, never underestimate the value of physical therapy or cosmetic surgery in helping to heal a grievous injury or overcome a serious accident. Although most insurance policies that cover this can be expensive, if you can afford it at all I'd recommend it.

When all is said and done, your choice of medical policy is determined by what you can afford. My advice is simple, try to afford the most you can. Medical insurance is the key lifeblood in modern living, as it effectively can extend your lifespan by decades. Remember, in the old days, people barely lived beyond 50 due to a lack of medical care, and could easily die in their 30s or 40s due to not treating a wound well; now, you can likely reach your 80s or even 90s with the help of good medicine; and any injuries you have in your 30s or 40s won't even affect you if treated well. Make sure you can afford it to live beyond your natural means, because if you can it will literally give you decades more life to live and make your life far more comfortable to live if things go wrong.

Next, we can talk about things like home insurance or car insurance. Since both represent major financial investments, both need to be insured. Remember, if you have no home, then you are homeless. There are many implications to this that can undoubtedly prevent you from accessing vital modern luxuries, like the internet, good food, eCommerce delivery, or a loan. Likewise, it can also have an impact on your ability to have and maintain a job if you have nowhere to wash yourself or your clothes; and can even have further knock-on effects in other avenues of your life. People who have no home often spiral downward simply because they have no "base of operations" from which to run their lives and uplift themselves. Their laptops and cell phones are more easily stolen, and they often cannot apply for things like insurance in the first place.

To that end, making sure you have a roof over your head is an absolute must. If you are low on funds you can rent a low-end apartment, bunk with a roommate, or even live in your mom's basement. Just keep yourself off the streets at all costs. More importantly, if you do decide to become a homeowner and get a home loan for $500,000, then make sure you ensure that house for as near to $500,000 as possible (preferably more) so that you can recover if it ever burns down and even afford another one thereafter.

Likewise, you cannot fill your house with a bunch of vital work equipment like an expensive sewing room, lathe, gaming laptop, or 3D printer that you use to work and *not* insure these items from theft or flooding. You have no idea how far it could set you back if you build a YouTube channel based on reviewing video games or painting figurines only for all the contents of your "creator space" to be carried out by a group of thugs. Even with insurance, your channel will be heavily set back as you spend a month to re-acquire all the things you've lost. The matter becomes far ruinous if your channel goes silent for a year causing you to lose a ton of momentum.

This principle becomes equally valid for all professions and business types. Business insurance during a riot, city fire, earthquake, or sinkhole may be the only thing that carries you through a disaster.

Thereafter, you can next consider car insurance. Cars are major financial investments that are often vital in some cases in order to work. In other words, if you cannot reach your workplace without a car, your car needs insurance.

Likewise, if you have kids, you need life insurance in the event you die, and someone needs to take care of them. Perhaps even funeral cover. The truth is, the more responsibilities you have, the more things you should consider insuring.

I'd like to recommend a small exercise. On the left, I want you to write down things that you need to survive or are dependent on for your survival, and on the right, we will write down an insurance policy that can cover it. On the top, we will write down our available budget, and on the bottom our projected costs.

Our goal is to write things down in terms of "priority" to sustain our lifestyle. In this exercise, begin by writing "my health" on the left, and then "health insurance" on the right. Write down a projected cost next to it. This item is often always first because no matter what lifestyle you live, it will be lost if your life fades. (There is one exception, which we will discuss shortly.)

Your next item will likely be your home insurance, this is because if you work a 9 to 5 job, you need a house to shower, eat, sleep, and relax when not at work. Preferably one with an internet connection. Likewise, if you are a content creator or a small business owner who runs a workshop out of the garage, you need a "home base" that can house all of your equipment safely. Thus, on the left, you will write "home" or "apartment" depending on your needs, and on the right the type of insurance. If you rent an apartment you only need insurance against theft, if you run a workshop in the garage your insurance needs will be far more robust. Again, write down your projected costs.

The only situation I can imagine where this won't be the second item is in the case of "digital nomads," who are often remote workers or influencers that prefer to constantly travel, usually house sitting in various different homes for extra cash, living in an Airbnb, or renting apartments in various cities as they move about. This is a niche lifestyle often also occupied by journalists, writers, musicians, and sometimes scientists, depending on the field they occupy.

In this niche context, your second most important item will be insurance for your laptop, or perhaps even "travel insurance." The medical scheme listed under our first priority item should also account for this lifestyle.

The third and fourth items will be far more dependent on your lifestyle. If you have a business, then it will likely be business insurance. If you need a car to get to work, it will be car insurance. If you own an ice cream truck, then you can choose between car or business insurance, and it will depend on what pays out the most and gets you the most "bang for your buck."

Furthermore, if you have kids or a spouse that changes things quite a bit. A house becomes more important. Life insurance may even claim the second priority spot, as having a medical scheme that covers your children fully becomes far more vital. Morbidly, perhaps if you have poor health and know you'll be gone in 2 years, life insurance to take care of your spouse and children can actually take the top priority spot, with a separate care package for your family second, and a specialized medical package for your "condition" third.

Take a pen and paper and go through the exercise on the next page and use it to grasp which insurance policies are vital to keep the wheels turning in case "everything" goes wrong. At the bottom, write the projected costs and compare them to your budget. You can consider removing the "least important" insurance packages first, and perhaps compromising on certain insurance packages second; choosing policies that aren't as fantastic, but at least afford you some cover.

## Insurance Planning Exercise

### Available Budget:

| Important asset: | Best insurance choice (With cost): |
|---|---|
| 1. | 1. |
| 2. | 2. |
| 3. | 3. |
| 4. | 4. |
| 5. | 5. |
| 6. | 6. |

### Cost:

\*\*\*

So I'd like to move away from insurance for now and shift into a talk on how you will go about financing the closing chapters of your years, and counterintuitively, I want to do it by talking about Social Security funding; and the reason why this is counter-intuitive, is because Social Security is a form of taxation, unique in the fact that it exists solely to protect the elderly and the disabled from abject poverty.

Now, it may bother you that I want to talk about retirement when you're likely quite young. However, you must understand that making plans to keep yourself comfortable in your final years is a goal you should be passively striving for throughout your youth because when you get older you won't be physically capable of taking care of yourself. In fact, even if you are healthy in your old age, you may not be legally able depending on your chosen career…

There is no worse fate for a person than to be an old man or woman begging on the streets, especially during the age when you are at your most fragile and in need of special care. Luckily, President Reagan understood this long ago, just before the Second World War, and set in motion his Social Security Act; which since then has been refined and perfected into a system that in 2022 put on average $1,614 into the pockets of 97% of elderly Americans each month (National Academy of Social insurance, 2022). This is a decent amount especially given that at this point you've (hopefully) already paid off a home and perhaps a car or two. More importantly, it represents effectively one of the only retirement vehicles available that matches yearly inflation rates. Meaning that no other retirement schemes out there will adjust the payable amount when inflation alters the value of money.

Furthermore, I want you to listen closely to me and understand that your future Social Security check shouldn't be your only income source at this point; if you were clever and started young, then you would have hopefully combined this check with one or two other retirement plans in order to have set yourself up to live an incredibly comfortable life. That way, your Social Security check can be combined with another to not only keep your head above water, but actually give you a chance at living a very opulent life. You'd be surprised how flexible your options for having some fun with this late stage funding can be; these Social Security payments can even be made to you if you're traveling abroad in certain countries, meaning that if you invest well, you can spend your old age traveling the world in luxury. Therefore, you shouldn't rest on your laurels and only expect to live off Social Security at old age; rather try and make yourself happy with a comfortable and exciting final chapter in your life.

The thing is, what most people don't realize is that only about 7% of Americans won't grow old enough to be able to benefit from a Social Security check (Kagan, 2019). This means 7% of people won't make it to the age of 62, which is when you can start collecting. Now, to some, this may be a cause for alarm as 7% is a rather high number, however, the more interesting part to me is the fact that 93% of us *will* make it to old age in this country. This means that as a young person now, you need to come to realize there is an incredibly good chance you'll live to see the year 2062, and you may live well into the year 2080 or perhaps even 2090.

I can assure you, that if virtual reality helmets get perfected and people spend their days doing all sorts of cool things in cyberspace, you will absolutely seethe with rage in the reality that you didn't invest in your retirement and can't afford to play with all the cool future-tech gadgets around you. You'll look on with jealousy as people use all sorts of sci-fi devices or interact with holographic Pokémon and you are forced to be a doorman at the local Walmart.

Do yourself a favor and don't let this happen to you.

You can start by making sure you keep your Social Security Card safe. It contains your Social Security Number, and each American is assigned one at birth. This number is vital for identifying you and preventing identity theft, so keep it secret. Just as importantly, it is a legal requirement for you to seek work and apply for benefits at said workplace, specifically signing up for a 401K. A 401K is simply the investment vehicle used to track your earnings toward Social Security.

How it works is as follows: In order to qualify for a Social Security check, you must meet the minimum age of 62 or be disabled, and have contributed to the Social Security fund for at least 10 years. The amount you are given is determined by the amount you contributed during your 35 most productive years.

To facilitate this, a 401K is effectively a type of tax that your workplace will stamp onto your check, however, uniquely it is also a type of workplace benefit. To elaborate: Your employer will stipulate in your contract that for every $10 you contribute to your Social Security fund, it will contribute $12 (or $16, or $18, or $10, etc.) normally these values are quite standard and dictated by various laws. In essence, a 401K is a type of workplace benefit that can guarantee a very luxurious retirement if it is generous. You see, if you contributed a lot of money to the Social Security fund and waited for the longest amount possible to cash in, which is 70, then the amount it grants can be quite significant and guarantee a comfortable retirement. A good 401K can sweeten this deal further by significantly boosting the amount of Social Security you are allowed to benefit from. Furthermore, if you become disabled or die as a primary breadwinner in your home, then you or your spouse can collect a Social Security check as well.

Now, as I mentioned, you ideally want to avoid a situation where a Social Security check is your only income at old age. Ideally, you should have also invested some money in property, have paid off a house or two so that you can become a landlord, and perhaps also have invested in other retirement schemes, of which there are many.

Indeed, there are myriads of investment firms who will ask you for a monthly contribution, similar to insurance, and use that money in various investment endeavors. The hope is that they choose wise investments that will inevitably balloon in value and result in profits for them and a comfortable retirement for you. These retirement funds are often low risk and don't backfire easily, so you can be rest assured it is worthwhile. Additionally, you can consider simply putting some money in a savings account and allowing compound interest to balloon the value it contains. You need not put a lot away each month, even a mere $15 can matter…the important part is that you start young so that the compound interest can take effect and give you a massive retirement plan.

Compound interest is something you'll likely have learned about in school; however, in case you didn't, the idea is that interest will be used to increase the amount you saved or invested, at which point the next interest calculation incorporates the previous interest quantity. In other words, compound interest is the act of applying interest onto previous interest payments, creating a situation where interest earnings increase exponentially.

This manner of making money can take some time to get rolling, however, if you are willing to put money away for a period longer than 5 years then the amount of return you can gain can be substantial. Although initial interest earnings can be as low as a few dollars, with time it can balloon to a few thousand per year, each year. In other words, putting a lump sum of cash away in your 20s can result in a large payout when you decide to retire in your 60s. Obviously, the more you can put away the more you will get to harvest when you're older. The important part, however, is that you start as early as possible in order to leverage the effects of compound interest. Just be mindful of scams, you need not partake in any elaborate retirement funds that some people advertise, as most banks have offerings that can see you well accommodated. I actually recommend using tried and true retirement vehicles rather than some "new" endeavors being clouted by some confident guy on a stage or a preppy website as being able to solve a ton of people's retirement problems.

In essence, you should only ever trust investment firms that have a long history and are considered reliable. Likewise, you should only ever trust banks that are well-trusted and have a long history.

A good rule of thumb to accept is that when something sounds too good to be true, it often is…life isn't fair, so often the most unfortunate option is also the least likely to be a scam.

# MAKING MAJOR
# FINANCIAL DECISIONS

It would be wonderful if we could coast through life without having to worry about things like debt, loans, leases, or financing schemes. Unfortunately, as most people grow up they eventually reach a point where they will need to make complex financial commitments in order to get through life. There was perhaps a time long ago when a loan need not be taken in order to finance something like a house or a car, however, unfortunately with time people who sold things like cars and houses came to understand they could ask for more and risk less by expecting loans to be taken out. Thus, the idea of taking out a loan and living in debt has to some extent become the financially normal way of living for almost all people.

To that end, you need to realize that one day you will likely need to get a loan in order to finance a few things in life that you want. That being said, just because it's normal doesn't mean it is wise. A loan is a complex financial decision that should be made with a lot of careful planning and realistic thinking. Most importantly, caution should be the prevailing state of mind throughout the entire process. Some banks will actually train their bankers to pressure you and say things like, "It's a standard contract that anyone signs," "My break is soon, we need to be quick," or even, "If you don't sign this now, we will only be able to process it by…" They may even want you to make some sort of signature in order to see the contract in the first place.

You need to understand that you have a few rights at play that you should ensure you enforce during these interactions. If you don't make the effort to stand up a bit for yourself then you may find yourself steamrolled by a banker who is trying to pressure you into signing up for policies that are not in your best interest.

For one, you are allowed to be fully informed of the contents of a contract before signing. This means that if a banker doesn't want to explain things to you, or doesn't want you to waste time reading and is trying to compel you to be quick in signing; then you have every right to tell them to wait as you read. If they disagree you can explain your rights to them and tell them you will first take your time to read and understand the contract before signing. Sometimes they may say that the contract is "strictly digital" and may not be printed for you to take home and read later, at which point you can explain to them that they need to email it to you since you have the right to read it without duress. If they try to give an explanation for why they can't then you can specifically explain to them why it is wrong, and tell them they'll need to leave you with the computer for two or three hours as you calmly read the contract and take notes. If they can't do that, then they'll need to make an appointment for you to sit and read at your own pace. Do not let anyone strongarm you into signing contracts quickly.

Second, you are actually allowed to alter a contract to suit you. Of course, the bank has a right to dispute or refuse these changes if it wants. Therefore, you need to realize that a bank signing is a type of negotiation. If you decide to scratch out the parts of the contract that require you to pay interest on a loan, effectively stating that you will pay no interest on a loan, then the bank will obviously outright refuse the contract. Of course, it may be more reasonable to slightly tweak things like the timeframe when you are expected to pay back, or perhaps see if you can't reduce the interest by 0.5% on a loan. Perhaps if the contract insists you are supposed to pay X each month, you can try and add a clause that you are allowed to miss a month, or perhaps pay slightly less during certain months. The main thing to understand is that many of the contracts the banks have people sign are heavily biased in their favor, and most people sign them since the banker looking at them will have an air of "this is the contract, take it or leave it." However, you technically do have the right to take the contract and alter it to suit your needs, if the banker on the other end of the table is willing to play ball, then you may be able to negotiate a contract for yourself that is a lot less one-sided in favor of the bank.

Bankers often have a host of strict rules they need to follow when negotiating and navigating these contracts, because of this you may find that they will be very inflexible in terms of how they go about allowing your attempts to negotiate. However, you need to understand that these contract rights you have are applicable to all major financial decisions you will ever face in life. So although the local banker may be hard pressed to allow you a 0.2% reduction in interest, and consider it a magnanimous concession of kindness that you may take a few months longer to repay a loan than is expected, the fact is a car salesman or real estate agent will not be equally as positioned to be strict during contract negotiations.

When it comes to contract negotiations for things like homes or cars, where the person on the other side of the table is often secretly quite eager for your signature due to being reliant on that signature for income, you'll find you have a lot more wiggle room for negotiations.

It may not be too far-fetched for you to ask a real estate agent for the contract, take it home, spend the weekend crossing out all the statements you don't like, and ask to have things added that you want by physically writing it in and returning it to the agent. The agent will likely be quite unhappy with this, but since there are often several hundreds of thousands of dollars at stake, they will likely end up approving most of your desired changes and requests, or price renegotiations — assuming they are within reason.

For example, let's say that you found a house that you really like, however the paint on the walls looks run down and the grass in the backyard looks dried out and dead in certain areas. You have every right to write into the contract that if you sign the contract and agree on the purchase, the previous owner is required to repaint the walls a certain color and replant the grass out of his own pocket 2 weeks before you move in. You could even say that if they do a poor job at painting then they owe you money or must pay for fixing their mistake. Once again, since there are often a few hundred thousand dollars at stake, you'd be surprised what people would be willing to agree to in order to get your signature here. You could even write in a clause that if a third-party contractor of your choice finds a few months later that there is severe damage to the home hidden beyond sight (rotten pillars, old pipes, etc.), then the previous owner is expected to pay for the repairs.

My point with all this is a rather simple one. As an adult, you need to understand that you need not be forced to sign contracts, especially those that revolve around major financial decisions, a contract should be approached on your own terms and handled with much foresight and planning. Especially a strong temperament of realism and resistance to your impulses.

Take the act of purchasing a car, for example. Many people will walk into a dealership without being quite certain what they want, making eye contact with a deluxe sports car far beyond their means, and often willingly agree to a financing scheme where they will be paying off debts for well over 6 years. Sometimes people will willingly get a loan in order to pay off a car meticulously over 8 to 9 years, perhaps even getting a balloon payment (which is effectively a second loan), simply to keep the monthly payment as low as possible for their dream car.

Does this sound wise?

It is entirely possible that by agreeing to a high-interest rate, large balloon payments, and agreeing to spend the next 10 years of your life paying it off, that you can get the monthly costs for your dream car down to a point where you can afford it, yet I can assure you, this is entirely the wrong choice.

To start, the chances are good you won't have the car 7 years later. I can't quite say what will happen...perhaps someone will hijack it. Perhaps you'll crash it. Perhaps you'll be caught with a DUI and have your license suspended. Perhaps even the car breaks down and fully seizes up for some reason. I don't know.

What I do know, is that it is entirely unreasonable to think that you can financially commit 10 years of your life to something that can be destroyed or removed from your life two months after signing all the papers: as easy as one, two, three.

Cars are inherently *terrible* investment options. To that end, the notion that a person can attempt to pay one off for any period longer than 5 years is considered by almost all financial experts to be a horrible decision. It is true that theoretically, you can take perfect care of a car for well over 8 years, avoiding all accidents, natural disasters, and events of crime.

But what statistically happens to most people is that their cars will, in one way or another, be removed from their life before reaching that point. What they are then left with is the financial burden of having to pay off a car they don't have while trying to afford a second.

Now obviously, a good insurance policy can circumvent this. However, even still, you are left with a situation where you have no equity with which to trade in the car and afford an upgrade, and you'll spend most of your life driving an "old" car. Never forget that ten years is a long time. By the time you've paid off your car, the entire world may have made a switch to electric vehicles, leaving you alone in the dust with a standard combustion engine in a world where gas prices are so high that people will pity you as they watch you count the dollars at the pump.

This is why you need to carefully consider the implications of any long-term major financial decisions very meticulously. You cannot predict the future, therefore, the faster you can get things paid off the better off you are going to be. It will leave you in a place where you can make more flexible decisions. In the above scenario, it would be wiser to buy a car you can comfortably afford, and that you are able to pay off before five years. Then, once the car is paid off, you can trade it in as equity in order to finance a well-upgraded dream car of your choice more easily, in a manner that once again won't destroy the bank or tie you down in the long run.

Then, five years later you can trade in your dream car as equity *again* in order to pay for an even more amazing car. Thus, ten years down the line from your first car purchase you'll be driving your hyper advance, AI-powered, electric supercar past some poor guy who still owns an ancient gas guzzler and is counting dollars at the pump; and it would have cost you less to do so over the years, *and* you would have been living more comfortably over the years. All you needed to do was be willing to accept a more modest car when you started out.

***

Similar philosophies are also at play when buying a house. Houses are major financial investments that can root you in a location over long periods of time. Therefore, you should only ever commit to buying one if you are certain you want to live somewhere permanently and have a good fighting chance at affording it.

There are entire books dedicated to purchasing homes out there, and for that reason, I won't go all too in-depth on the topic. However, what I can offer is some quick-fire advice.

To start, if it's too good to be true, then it probably is.

If a seller or realtor is offering you a property at a price far below what is considered average for such a property, or the area itself, why? There is undoubtedly a reason that is being kept beyond your sight and tactfully unmentioned as you are shown the luxurious garden and marble finishings.

In the popular TV show *How I Met Your Mother*, the happy-go-lucky couple Lily and Marshall find their dream apartment at a price beyond their greatest hopes. They, therefore, do not hesitate to buy as soon as possible, fearing the realtor's warnings that other couples are also interested.

The outcome?

Living in the new home is initially exactly as expected: a dream. The loving couple enjoys their new home and invites their friends over to bask in their good fortune with them. Yet as soon as one of their friends steps foot in the living room, he remarks: "The floor is skewed."

Of course, Lily and Marshall initially shoot the remark down, assuming that the observation is an exaggeration. Yet with time, they begin to notice that the floor is indeed tilted at an angle...if they were to leave objects lying around that had a curved bottom, like a ball, then they would be able to observe it rolling. With time, the awareness of how severely tilted their floor began to set in as they could see all their furniture leaning to the side, and they begin to panic that their children will grow up lopsided with one leg shorter than the other as they are forced to eternally walk upon a skew plain... to add salt to the wound, the contractors they consult assure them fixing the problem would be incredibly expensive.

As the young couple sits on their couch contemplating their poor fortune, leaning to the side against gravity as the couch hangs slanted on the floor, a smell wafts through the room more dire and potent than any they had smelt before... it is an odor so ghastly it chokes and overwhelms them to the point that they forget for a moment that their floors are not level. Turns out, their new home is situated near a sewage treatment plant that was temporarily shut down for a few months due to maintenance...

This example I offer you may be a comedic TV overdramatization. Yet, it is a joke borne from the stories of many people who had jumped giddily at an attractive price and a grandiose presentation without doing an investigative check first. Had Lilly and Marshall spent some time talking to the neighbors first or driving around the area, they'd have known about the sewage plant. If they had hired an independent investigator or at least asked their friends to come to look at the house also, they would've known about the floor.

Therefore, the first shred of advice I'd like to give you is to inspect not only the home fully but also the surrounding area as well as your neighbors. Make sure to involve your spouse and anyone you trust in order to gain their insight. Furthermore, a competent real estate agent who you trust and who will give you good advice can go a long way in helping you find a good home. Realtors can be a powerful ally or an insidious enemy depending on your choice, so review several of them first before choosing one for your journey. Furthermore, make sure to consult the lender first so that you have a pre-approved loan, which will help you be more aware of what you can afford. It will also be worth your time to hire an inspector to fully investigate the building before making a purchase. The more you pre-arm yourself with knowledge and surround yourself with trustworthy and competent people, the wiser your purchase decision will be.

The next piece of advice I'd like to give you is to be aware of the hidden costs of purchasing a property. Trust me, there are many.

To start, the costs of the real estate agent as well as the property inspector are something to account for as you will be needing their consistent help from the start of the process well into the closing moments of the deal and perhaps even a few months after you move in. These people are worth getting and to that end, you need to budget for their services in addition to your home. Furthermore, you'll find that there are a variety of home registration fees involved in the actual purchasing process, as well as what is known as a "down payment." This is a cash value you are expected to give upfront and is often determined by the lender who is offering you your mortgage. For first-time homebuyers who have a good credit score, this can be as low as 3%. But be wary, because 3% of $400,000 is still $16,000, which can be a lot of money for some people to provide upfront.

Next, you need to be aware that there are also "closing costs," which are a series of costs you are expected to pay in order to fully transfer the property (In essence, they are admin costs.) Sometimes, you can request that the seller assist you with these, however, your ability to do so will depend on if your mortgage provider supports it and the amount the seller may assist with is determined by the lender as well.

Close on the heels of the closing costs we find that there are also costs associated with getting set up. These will be the costs you need to pay for the moving company to move all your furniture, repairmen services to fix anything you later discover is broken (which I assure you will happen), costs for setting up things like security systems and internet connections, perhaps you may find you'll also need to hire several services you didn't anticipate prior to moving in. I can assure you these costs build up quickly and happen almost every time. As discussed above, you can try and negotiate a contract where the seller must cover these things if they pop up, but what you wrote in may not cover all that you'll need to fix, maintain, or alter in your new home as you get yourself set up.

Lastly, there are further hidden costs in the form of rates and taxes that you'll often need to pay monthly along with the down payments on your mortgage, which you'll need to budget for. You should also note that effectively all mortgage providers require you to get the insurance that protects your home from things like fire, which should be enough to completely rebuild it if it was destroyed and will add to the monthly cost of your home.

If you take a moment to reread everything that I just listed, you'll no doubt conclude that hidden costs are a major component of a property purchase and that you need a ton of money in the bank before you can go about trying to purchase a home. To this end, I recommend you only take this step when you are financially secure, to begin with.

Thus, the process of buying a home by lending money is as follows:

First, make sure you have a lot of money saved up to cover as many of the hidden purchasing costs as possible.

Then, go to a bank or other lender and ask for pre-approval for a home mortgage. This pre-approval will give you a good idea of what sort of price range is acceptable.

Next, interview several realtors and ask about their experience as well as which areas they cover. Providing them with your pre-approval letter will help them select a good home for you.

Fourth, investigate several homes together with your realtor and take your time to fully understand the surrounding area, the people that will be your community, as well as what sort of economy fuels an area. In my own opinion, knowing where a town gets its money is a good way to determine what it will be like 30 years later. A town that relies on tourism for wealth is inherently risky, as this can fluctuate seasonally and if the town loses tourist attractiveness (which can happen quite arbitrarily and sporadically), then property values may plummet. Likewise, a town that relies on the timber industry may bankrupt itself, unless the tree plantations are maintained sustainably and continuously replanted…therefore, a town that has two to three "sources" of money is almost always a safe bet.

Fifth, take some time to deeply inspect the home and ask the seller for past electrical, gas, and water bills. Make sure the building you see physically matches what is registered with the blueprint and homeowner association, including outside cottages, pools, and sheds. Ask questions about the age of the plumbing, electrical, and roof. Hire an inspector to investigate the home fully and walk with him as he tries to determine that there is no hidden water damage or toxic substances present.

Sixth, you can begin negotiations on the price to pay for a home. This will be mostly determined by what you know you can afford from your pre-approval letter as well as your common sense. Remember that you'll have hidden costs beyond the monthly payments being discussed as you do so. In a seller's market, prices can jump during bidding, and you may be tempted to punch above your weight in order to claim the home (which you shouldn't). To counter this, rather look at houses that are below your budget so that you can punch high when prices go up during the bidding process. Likewise, during a buyer's market, you may have the luxury to look at the higher end of the price range as it will be unlikely for the price to jump a lot.

Seventh, you can seek final approval from the lender for a mortgage. A mortgage is essentially just a term used to describe a home loan and comes with unique rules and properties that make it unique from other loans. Such as having insurance expectations as well as unique repossession rights for the lender offering you a mortgage. It is also possible to get a second mortgage on a home if things aren't going well, but you'd rather want to avoid this. Generally, mortgages are fixed over periods like 30 years.

Eight, buy the house and move in. What happens here will depend strongly on what was negotiated and planned up to this point. As mentioned, there will be closing costs and various hidden fees in the form of hiring landscapers to plant a garden or remove something from the property. Regardless of what happens here, just be aware it will cost a lot of extra money.

Ninth, make sure you meet every mortgage payment as it arrives. The best way to do this is to make sure you have some money tucked away in advance so that you will be able to pay even when you can't work for a few months (remember COVID?) Furthermore, a life insurance policy can help your family cover these costs and keep their home when you become grievously injured or you die. The main problem here is that if you fail to pay your mortgage, it will become quite hard to get another or move to a new home as it will have a poor effect on your future credit ratings. So rather save yourself a ton of heartache by avoiding the act of over-committing on a home you can barely afford.

# TAKING LIFE
# BY THE HORNS

I must admit, I know all this talk about mortgages, insurance, careers, and the like can be scary. The truth is a lot of people don't feel ready. The truth is a lot of the adults around you that you see paying mortgages and worrying about insurance still aren't sure they were ever ready.

The act of taking on responsibility is scary...mistakes happen, and people make them so easily. We all inherently know this and as a result, I think a lot of people wait until the very last second before jumping in and accepting their responsibilities, sometimes only ever deciding to do it out of a sense of duty, or often because they had no choice. In my own case, the best way I could go about conquering my own shortcomings and managing all my responsibilities, lied in taking control of my own life. In Chapter 4 I undergo a lot of effort to explain to you an exercise where you seek to define your archetype. I am aware that to many, the exercise may seem silly, but the thing is that if you don't take the time to really reflect and write down what your moves should be, chances are good you won't start making any moves until you're forced to. In this way, a lot of people inevitably become stuck in the rat race and live a life of reacting to things, rather than anticipating them and moving toward their own goals.

These self-evaluation exercises I've been showing you in this book, and employing in my own life, became a tool that I could use to navigate the world in a way that gave me some fulfillment and the sense that I can not only contribute to the world around me, but actively become a positive force in it that can uplift my family, my community, and my country. The days of me meandering about in search of purpose are behind me, and in its place I was able to find a niche for myself in the world where I know I am doing good, and I know I have something to teach others.

Because of this, I previously compiled a list of exercises into my other book: *Pantheria Life Log,* and started selling it on Amazon. Not because I needed the money, but because I wish somebody could have just helped me navigate my life as well when I was younger. This previous book is effectively a dairy and day planner designed to help people orient their goals and plan the steps they should take to reach them much like what was done in Chapter 4, yet to a far more consistent, functional, and practical extent.

Yet when I reflected on this diary, I came to realize that some people may fail to grasp just how powerful the simple effort of getting your act together can actually be in shaping your life and giving you a fighting chance at living a life worth living.

Thus, I chose to write this book, so that people, especially those who have not yet realized just how serious the great game can be, can reflect on the things that matter and use my prior work *Pantheria life log* to navigate the chaos that is life.

When we are young, we often tend to think adulthood is something that just "happens" to you when you get old enough, and in an act of great humor, life tends to do *exactly* that to us. Adulthood indeed does become something that just *happens* to you, quite inevitably so.

And tragically…since we never see it coming, and often only realize we must swim once we can't feel the safe floor of the shallow shore beneath our feet, we often panic, flail, and make the wrong choices in a desperate attempt to avoid drowning; or perhaps even cast the dire thought into our hearts that we *did* something wrong long ago, and are now suffering for it, unable to reverse our inevitable inhalation of water.

No.

In truth, you need not panic to keep your head above water. This book was written as a reminder to you that you can indeed take action and rise above the danger that surrounds you, and do whatever you want. Sure…taxes, loans, careers, and bravery are all serious matters, yet you need not fear them. They become minor things when you choose to grasp them of your own accord, and they become tools that you can manipulate when you decide to use the teachings of this book to own them.

Indeed, I want you to do the exercises in this book, for the sake alone of knowing where you must go next. Many things in life can be big and scary, but they are easy to face when we define them, break them into small manageable steps, and take each step patiently and with curiosity, again and again.

How does one eat an elephant? One bite at a time, while improving your chew each time.

That is what I want you to take away from this work, and why I previously created the *Life Log*, so that we can incrementally track our improvements.

Now, I ask that you strap in and prepare for the rollercoaster that will be your life. In this world, you will likely be tasked to change course often and seek new dreams as you realize old ones must fade. This will be one of the greater challenges a person will ever face and a fate that awaits us all. Few people wind up doing what they set out to do in their youth, lesser still are those that live a life without unexpected events derailing their course completely.

The truth is that although the purpose of this book was to help you plan ahead for your life, chances are good nothing will go as planned.

Fear not. Success is the application of effort in the same direction.

This means that if you want to reach your goals, you must first understand what those goals are; understand what must be done to reach them; and find ways to perform those steps even though life does a variety of things to stop you.

You must be patient in your pursuit of the things you want, in my own experience, I found that when I pursue new goals or try to build new habits, it often takes 24 months to get anywhere and have things settle well for me. This means it is more important to acknowledge the value of each small step you take than to seek fulfillment in the acquisition of the goals you set for yourself.

Furthermore, I must impress on you a truth I was fortunate enough to realize in my own life.

It is easy to worry.

It is easier to complain.

It is easiest to accept victimhood.

The world is now filled with those who point around them at all that is wrong and say:

"Because of this, we cannot do."

"We are oppressed."

"Tragedy has befallen us, because of this we are less and cannot compete"

"What hope do we have if the world is structured like this?"

These people often display a variety of very valid arguments on why things cannot be done, why there is oppression, why some are victims, and why the tragedies in their lives hold them back.

Yet these people also seem to intrinsically fail at grasping the point…

Life is cruel.

It is unfair.

Many structures will exist that prevent people from achieving their potential — even when we keep tearing them down, many people will be oppressed, many will face dire tragedy and setbacks, and the world is indeed sometimes structured to contest us.

Yet heroes and victors are those who choose to enjoy life *despite* this, they choose to laugh and strike forth *regardless* of inevitable setbacks, they'll choose to do something even if there are barriers, they find a way to overcome oppression, they find a way to overcome tragedy, and they find a way to forgive or ignore those who made their lives hard.

Indeed, they seek to live the life of a happy person who enjoys what they have and stands proudly for what they care for no matter what happens or happened to them, often becoming an inspiration in the process...

The key to achieving this high level of magic has nothing to do with being an amazing person. It has everything to do with not overindulging in self-pity.

When you walk down the street and stub your toe, you can choose to be upset about it for a day and complain in the ear of all who walk by; or you can allow yourself to say, "Ow!" a few times before perhaps giving a laugh and walking on.

The key to becoming a force of strength and positivity lies in not allowing the setbacks to "matter" much. Sure... if someone bullied you, you could indeed think, *Wow, being bullied was awful*, and you may even allow yourself to feel hurt about it.

Yet, you must never go "I was bullied because something is wrong with me," or "I deserved it."

Or even worse…

"Since I was bullied as a child, I am now insecure and fragile. I am broken."

"The way people treated me messed me up."

Never think like that.

Never allow the tragedy of your past to define you.

Tragedy happens. Tragedy sucks and the pain it leaves is real. But when you allow it to become a part of you then you let go of the parts of you that you can feel good about, and you inevitably become a person with a victim mentality.

You see, the key to operating as a secure, well-rounded, adult who pursues their goals and takes care of those around them, is to not let bad moments become bad days, and not allow bad events to become a bad life. This rule has helped me overcome great hardship in my own life. I could have easily given up and whined about the tragedy that is my life when I lost a scholarship, or when my record label failed, or when I and my first wife divorced. Yet years later, I'm a happy father, a happy husband to a good woman, and proud member of the US Navy with a tertiary qualification of my choice, simply because I was wise enough to not hang onto my own misfortunes.

# Your Feedback Counts

### Please, leave a REVIEW
### wherever you made your purchase.

Share your experience with
others help us grow our audience.

 Booksprout

**For the opportunity to read advanced copies of our
books, join our review team on BookSprout:**

**https://booksprout.co/reviewer/team/
31264/panterax-book-review-team**

# Conclusion

Now that you're a functional Adult, let's work on being a mature Adult.

This book was designed to lay the foundation for becoming a functional adult, meaning this will help guide you to do the bare minimum to make it day to day, but it is not an automatic fast track to success in your career, social circles, or life. Success in life is more than accumulating money, awards, and followers, and you are not guaranteed those things just by being a basic, solid adult.

You will, however, have the tools to maintain your life while you develop the more advanced skills to create the type of success you desire. This is a lifelong process requiring many skills and lessons. Maturity involves the ability to resolve conflict within yourself, with your environment, and with others: to not only navigate life, but improve life in a way that is fulfilling to you and those around you. Life is about people and how you impact them.

The greatest life we can live is a life lived for others.

Those who don't grasp this are destined to live meaningless lives no matter how they try to trick themselves.

If you attend any funeral you will hear how the dead impacted the living. You will not or rarely hear about how much money was made, how responsible they were, or how they always followed or broke the rules...

You will hear about how their actions impacted others and how those actions helped influence another's life. The only thing that lives beyond us is the love we left with others, and the only way to truly express that love rests in being able to seize control of your life.

There is a stoic quote about how we die twice: the day we die, and the day the last person that knew us dies. So keep your impact on the lives of others in mind when thinking about how you will develop as an adult and strive for your own vision of success and happiness.

If you found anything in this book valuable to you, I implore you to go onto Amazon and leave me a nice review. You'd be surprised how many thousands of people will buy and enjoy this book before a single nice review is said; meanwhile, each and every person who may disagree slightly with my book will likely leave several scathing comments in a fit of rage.

You can help spread the message of this work and assist others in their journey to adulthood simply by opening your browser and saying something nice.

# PANTHERIA LIFE LOGS BY PANTERAX

## *Available on Amazon.com*

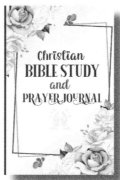

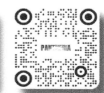

# References

Abhinandhinee. (2022, April 4). *Netflix | The success story of the subscription streaming service*. Failure before Success. https://failurebeforesuccess.com/netflix/

Abt, S. (2019). Lance Armstrong, Biography, Tour de France, Doping, & Facts. In *Encyclopædia Britannica*. https://www.britannica.com/biography/Lance-Armstrong

Ackerman, C. (2018, July 12). *What is Self-Acceptance? 25 Exercises + Definition and Quotes*. PositivePsychology.com. https://positivepsychology.com/self-acceptance/

Andrews, E. (2015, August 28). *5 Famous Pyrrhic Victories*. HISTORY. https://www.history.com/news/5-famous-pyrrhic-victories

Ashley, E. (2019, January 4). *10 Common Budgeting Mistakes and How to Avoid Them*. Mint Notion. https://www.mintnotion.com/budgeting/common-budgeting-mistakes/

Baldwin, H. W. (2020, July 30). *America at War: Victory in the Pacific*. Www.foreignaffairs.com. https://www.foreignaffairs.com/articles/united-states/1945-10-01/america-war-victory-pacific#:~:text=The%20greatest%20war%20in%20which

Bank of America. (2021). *How to File Your Own Taxes: 6 Steps for Beginners*. Better Money Habits. https://bettermoneyhabits.bankofamerica.com/en/taxes-income/how-to-file-your-taxes-in-your-20s

Barnato, K. (2015, July 16). *Did the fall of the Berlin Wall help end Apartheid?* CNBC; CNBC. https://www.cnbc.com/2015/07/16/did-the-fall-of-the-berlin-wall-help-end-apartheid.html

Bauwer, N. (2012, November 6). *Top South African cyclist bust for doping.* The Mail & Guardian. https://mg.co.za/article/2012-11-06-top-sa-cyclist-david-george-bust-for-doping/

Bechard, A. (2016, January 21). *How to Stop Trying to Fit In and Finally Belong.* Tiny Buddha. https://tinybuddha.com/blog/how-to-stop-trying-to-fit-in-and-finally-belong/

Biography.com Editors. (2018, January 4). *Lance Armstrong.* Biography. https://www.biography.com/athlete/lance-armstrong

Bluestone, C. D. (2005). Humans are born too soon: impact on pediatric otolaryngology. *International Journal of Pediatric Otorhinolaryngology, 69*(1), 1–8. https://doi.org/10.1016/j.ijporl.2004.07.021

Bradford, A. (2016, March 2). *Kangaroo Facts.* Live Science; Live Science. https://www.livescience.com/27400-kangaroos.html

Bregman, P. (2016, March 8). *5 Steps to Investing Your Energy More Wisely.* Harvard Business Review. https://hbr.org/2016/03/5-steps-to-investing-your-energy-more-wisely

Bregman, R. (2020, May 9). The real Lord of the Flies: what happened when six boys were shipwrecked for 15 months. *The Guardian.* https://www.theguardian.com/books/2020/may/09/the-real-lord-of-the-flies-what-happened-when-six-boys-were-shipwrecked-for-15-months

Cassata, C. (2021, September 25). *Flaws and All: How to Accept Yourself in 8 Steps.* Psych Central. https://psychcentral.com/lib/ways-to-accept-yourself

Cassella, C. (2021, December). *Scientists Have Finally Discovered Why The Brain Consumes So Much Energy, Even at Rest.* ScienceAlert. https://www.sciencealert.com/a-hidden-structure-in-our-neurons-could-explain-why-the-brain-guzzles-so-much-energy

Casserly, M. (2011, January). *Multiple Personalities And Social Media: The Many Faces of Me.* Forbes. https://www.forbes.com/sites/meghancasserly/2011/01/26/multiple-personalities-and-social-media-the-many-faces-of-me/?sh=6dbbc5bd6d51

Center of budget and policy priorities. (2020, August 13). *Policy Basics: Top Ten Facts about Social Security.* Center on Budget and Policy Priorities. https://www.cbpp.org/research/social-security/top-ten-facts-about-social-security

Cherry, K. (2022, February 14). *The Five Levels of Maslow's Hierarchy of Needs.* Verywellmind. https://www.verywellmind.com/what-is-maslows-hierarchy-of-needs-4136760

Church, M. (2022, April). *How to Think Laterally.* WikiHow. https://www.wikihow.com/Think-Laterally

Cole, B. M. (2019, March). *10 Reasons Why Networking Is Essential For Your Career.* Forbes. https://www.forbes.com/sites/biancamillercole/2019/03/20/why-networking-should-be-at-the-core-of-your-career/?sh=6006339f1300

Collatz, A. (2019, January). *The Difference Between a Lease and a Rental Agreement | SmartMove.* Www.mysmartmove.com. https://www.mysmartmove.com/SmartMove/blog/difference-between-lease-and-rental-agreement.page

Corporate Finance Institute. (2019). *Lease - Definition, Common Types of Leases, Examples.* Corporate Finance Institute. https://corporatefinanceinstitute.com/resources/knowledge/other/lease/

Daily, B. (2021, September). *TikTok's Dissociative Identity Disorder Community Is Going Viral — But Not Everyone's Happy About It*. BuzzFeed. https://www.buzzfeed.com/daily/tiktok-dissociative-identity-disorder-did-mental-health

David. (2021, April 20). *Help for those who feel like they don't fit in anywhere - Meaningful Paths*. Meaningful Paths. https://www.meaningfulpaths.com/2021/04/20/dont-fit-in-anywhere/

Domning, D. (2018, May). Opinion | Because of evolution, we all are born premature. *Washington Post*. https://www.washingtonpost.com/opinions/because-of-evolution-we-are-all-born-premature/2018/05/11/21c119d0-5323-11e8-a6d4-ca1d035642ce_story.html

Eatough. (2021). *How to Create a Life Plan (a Life Planning Template)*. Betterup.com. https://www.betterup.com/blog/life-planning

Eatough, E. (2021, December 21). *What Is Networking and Why Is It So Important?* Www.betterup.com. https://www.betterup.com/blog/networking#:~:text=Networking%20contributes%20to%20your%20social

Fisher, J. F. (2019, December 27). *How to get a job often comes down to one elite personal asset, and many people still don't realize it*. CNBC. https://www.cnbc.com/2019/12/27/how-to-get-a-job-often-comes-down-to-one-elite-personal-asset.html

Gärdenfors, P. (2006). Thinking from an evolutionary perspective. *How Homo Became Sapiens*, 1–23. https://doi.org/10.1093/acprof:oso/9780198528517.003.0001

Giedinghagen, A. (2022). The tic in TikTok and (where) all systems go: Mass social media induced illness and Munchausen's by internet as explanatory models for social media associated abnormal illness behavior. *Clinical Child Psychology and Psychiatry*, 135910452210985. https://doi.org/10.1177/13591045221098522

Gillig, P. M. (2019). Dissociative identity disorder: a controversial diagnosis. Psychiatry (Edgmont (Pa. : Township)), 6(3), 24–29. https://www.ncbi.nlm.nih.gov/pmc/articles/PMC2719457/

Golen, T., & Ricciotti, H. (2021, July 1). *Does exercise really boost energy levels?* Harvard Health. https://www.health.harvard.edu/exercise-and-fitness/does-exercise-really-boost-energy-levels

Greek travelers. (2020, June). *300: Movie Vs. Reality.* Greektraveltellers. com. https://greektraveltellers.com/blog/300-beyond-the-movie#:~:text=Like%20the%20comic%20book%2C%20the

H & R Block. (2017, June 14). *How Much Do You Have To Make To File Taxes?* H&R Block. https://www.hrblock.com/tax-center/income/other-income/how-much-do-you-have-to-make-to-file-taxes/#:~:text=In%202021%2C%20for%20example%2C%20the

Harvard Health Publishing. (2019). *Eating to boost energy - Harvard Health.* Harvard Health; Harvard Health. https://www.health.harvard.edu/healthbeat/eating-to-boost-energy

Heart, D. (2022, February 18). *(Masterclass) The Hidden Secrets Behind Netflix's Success.* ThePowerMBA. https://www.thepowermba.com/en/blog/netflix-success

Herculano-Houzel, S. (2020, November). *Your big brain makes you human – count your neurons when you count your blessings.* The Conversation. https://theconversation.com/your-big-brain-makes-you-human-count-your-neurons-when-you-count-your-blessings-127398

Heyes, C. (2012). New thinking: the evolution of human cognition. *Philosophical Transactions of the Royal Society B: Biological Sciences, 367*(1599), 2091–2096. https://doi.org/10.1098/rstb.2012.0111

Higuera, V. (2017, August 9). *17 Biggest Budgeting Mistakes You're Making.* GOBankingRates. https://www.gobankingrates.com/saving-money/budgeting/biggest-budgeting-mistakes-youre-making/

Hopsicker, K. (2022, April). *9 tips to help you find your first job — and nail the interview.* CNBC. https://www.cnbc.com/2022/04/25/9-tips-to-help-you-find-your-first-job-and-nail-the-interview.html

Horsewill, I. (2021, January 21). *Netflix a success story of our times as it no longer needs to borrow money.* The CEO Magazine. https://www.theceomagazine.com/business/management-leadership/netflix/

Indeed editorial team. (2020, November 25). *How to Make a Life Plan in 6 Steps.* Indeed Career Guide. https://www.indeed.com/career-advice/career-development/how-to-make-a-life-plan

IRS. (2022). *Topic No. 409 Capital Gains and Losses | Internal Revenue Service.* Www.irs.gov. https://www.irs.gov/taxtopics/tc409#:~:text=Capital%20Gain%20Tax%20Rates

Jay, R. (2018, September 28). *7 Things Every First-Time Job Seeker Should Know.* FlexJobs Job Search Tips and Blog. https://www.flexjobs.com/blog/post/things-every-first-time-job-seeker-should-know/

Johnstone, R., & Manica, A. (2011). Evolution of personality differences in leadership. *Proceedings of the National Academy of Sciences, 108*(20), 8373–8378. https://doi.org/10.1073/pnas.1102191108

Jonas, J. (n.d.). *The Twelve Archetypes.* https://www.uiltexas.org/files/capitalconference/Twelve_Character_Archetypes.pdf

Kagan, J. (2019). *Social Security.* Investopedia. https://www.investopedia.com/terms/s/socialsecurity.asp

Kids Help Phone. (2018, June 19). *10 ways to practice self-acceptance.* Kids Help Phone. https://kidshelpphone.ca/get-info/10-ways-practice-self-acceptance/

Kozlowski, T. (2019, November 5). *It's Okay Not to Fit In.* Terri Kozlowski. https://terrikozlowski.com/its-okay-not-to-fit-in/

Kumar, B. (2022, February 18). *How To Make Money on YouTube in 2022 (7 Effective Ways).* Shopify. https://www.shopify.com/za/blog/198134793-how-to-make-money-on-youtube#1

Living with lions. (2022). *How To Age Lions | Mara Predator Project.* Livingwithlions.org. http://livingwithlions.org/mara/how-to/age-lions/#:~:text=Adult%20lions%20are%20between%203

Marquand, B. (2022, September). *14 Tips for First-Time Home Buyers.* NerdWallet. https://www.nerdwallet.com/article/mortgages/tips-for-first-time-home-buyers

Martin, M. (2022, January 23). Why the nature of TikTok could exacerbate a worrisome social media trend. *NPR.org.* https://www.npr.org/2022/01/23/1075216842/why-the-nature-of-tiktok-could-exacerbate-a-worrisome-social-media-trend

Mateo. (2015, April 17). *What is Your Psychological Archetype? [Free Test].* LonerWolf. https://lonerwolf.com/psychological-archetype-test/

Mayo Client. (2021, September 21). *7 great reasons why exercise matters.* Mayo Clinic. https://www.mayoclinic.org/healthy-lifestyle/fitness/in-depth/exercise/art-20048389#:~:text=Exercise%20boosts%20energy&text=Regular%20physical%20activity%20can%20improve

Mcleod, S. (2007). Maslow's Hierarchy of Needs. *Www.simplypsychology.org.* https://www.simplypsychology.org/maslow.html#:~:text=There%20are%20five%20levels%20in

Mcleod, S. (2018). *Carl Jung | Simply Psychology*. Simplypsychology.org. https://www.simplypsychology.org/carl-jung.html

Mengle, R. (2022, September 20). *What Are the Income Tax Brackets for 2022 vs. 2021?* Kiplinger. https://www.kiplinger.com/taxes/tax-brackets/602222/income-tax-brackets#:~:text=When%20it%20comes%20to%20federal

Moeller, K. (2017, May 12). *Human Animal Differences | Ask A Biologist*. Asu.edu. https://askabiologist.asu.edu/questions/human-animal-differences

Montiglio, P.-O., Ferrari, C., & Réale, D. (2013). Social niche specialization under constraints: personality, social interactions and environmental heterogeneity. *Philosophical Transactions of the Royal Society B: Biological Sciences, 368*(1618). https://doi.org/10.1098/rstb.2012.0343

Myriam Webster. (2022). *What is a "Pyrrhic victory"?* Www.merriam-Webster.com. https://www.merriam-webster.com/words-at-play/pyrrhic-victory-meaning#:~:text=A%20pyrrhic%20victory%20is%20a

Nantz, T. (2019, November 12). *12 Character Archetypes to Help You Create Your Heroes*. Jerry Jenkins | Proven Writing Tips. https://jerryjenkins.com/character-archetypes/

National Academy of Social insurance. (2022). *What is Social Security?* National Academy of Social Insurance. https://www.nasi.org/learn/social-security/what-is-social-security/

Nelson Mandela Foundation. (2022). *The Communist Threat - The O'Malley Archives*. Omalley.nelsonmandela.org. https://omalley.nelsonmandela.org/omalley/index.php/site/q/03lv02424/04lv02730/05lv03005/06lv03132/07lv03160.htm

Nettle, D. (2006). The Evolution of Personality Variation in Humans and Other Animals. *American Psychologist, 61*(6). https://doi.org/10.1037/0003-066X.61.6.622

News, N. (2022, April 12). *How the Human Brain Evolved to Harness Abstract Thought.* Neuroscience News. https://neurosciencenews.com/brain-evolution-abstract-thought-20364/

Old Mutual. (2017). *6 Tips for Buying a House for the First Time | Old Mutual.* Oldmutual.co.za. https://www.oldmutual.co.za/articles/6-tips-for-first-time-home-buyers

Oliver, M. (2017, August 5). *This Is Why Human Babies Take So Much Longer To Develop Than Most Animals.* Fatherly. https://www.fatherly.com/health-science/human-babies-born-helpless

Orchid. (2016, March 24). *5 Ways to Use Your Energy More Wisely.* Orchid Recovery Center. https://www.orchidrecoverycenter.com/blog/5-ways-to-use-your-energy-more-wisely/

PBS. (2022). *The Costs of War | American Experience | PBS.* Www.pbs.org. https://www.pbs.org/wgbh/americanexperience/features/pacific-costs-war/

Pope, B. R. (2022, June). *Character Archetypes: 14 That Matter for Writing (+ tips).* Self-Publishingschool.com. https://self-publishingschool.com/character-archetypes/

PsychAlive. (2015, August 28). *Finding Yourself: a Guide to Finding Your True Self.* PsychAlive. https://www.psychalive.org/finding-yourself/

Ramirez, M. (2021, December 21). *How to Make Money on Instagram: 5 Ways for 2022.* NerdWallet. https://www.nerdwallet.com/article/finance/how-to-make-money-on-instagram#:~:text=With%20just%201%2C000%20or%20so

Raphael, D. (2021 6). *The Do's and Don'ts of Eating for Energy*. Hospital for Special Surgery. https://www.hss.edu/article_eating-for-energy.asp

Raypole, C. (2020, June 11). *9 Ways To Kick Off Your Self-Discovery Journey*. Healthline. https://www.healthline.com/health/self-discovery#takeaway

Réale, D., & Dingemanse, N. J. (2010). Personality and individual social specialisation. *Social Behaviour*, 417–441. https://doi.org/10.1017/cbo9780511781360.033

Rodriguez, D. (2018, February 5). *Why Exercise Boosts Mood and Energy | Everyday Health*. EverydayHealth.com. https://www.everydayhealth.com/fitness/workouts/boost-your-energy-level-with-exercise.aspx

Rowland, S. (2007, May 12). *Experience: I convinced myself I was going mad*. The Guardian. https://www.theguardian.com/lifeandstyle/2007/may/12/healthandwellbeing.features

Rutger Bregman, Manton, E., & Moore, E. (2020). *Humankind : a hopeful history*. Bloomsbury Publishing.

Rutherford, A. (2018, September 21). *The human league: what separates us from other animals?* The Guardian; The Guardian. https://www.theguardian.com/books/2018/sep/21/human-instinct-why-we-are-unique

Saks, B. (2022). *United States - Individual - Taxes on personal income*. Taxsummaries.pwc.com. https://taxsummaries.pwc.com/united-states/individual/taxes-on-personal-income

Sander, V. (2021, March 10). *What To Do If You Don't Fit In (Practical Tips)*. SocialSelf. https://socialself.com/blog/not-fitting-in/

Securian financial. (2022). *How does compound interest work?* Securian Financial. https://www.securian.com/insights-tools/articles/how-compound-interest-works.html

Shakespeare, W. (1603). *Hamlet.*

Sloan, P. (2012a, April). *The Top Ten Lateral Thinking Puzzles.* Destination Innovation. https://www.destination-innovation.com/the-top-ten-lateral-thinking-puzzles/

Sloan, P. (2012b, April 1). *Top Ten Lateral Thinking Puzzles - the Answers.* Destination Innovation. https://www.destination-innovation.com/top-ten-lateral-thinking-puzzles-the-answers/

Socrates. (n.d.). *Socrates Quotes (Author of Apología de Sócrates).* Goodreads.com. https://www.goodreads.com/author/quotes/275648.Socrates

Stemmet, J., & Senekal, B. (2013). Threats of Communist expansion in Apartheid South Africa: NP claims versus CIA intelligence perspectives in the years 1960 to 1990. In North West University Repository. https://repository.nwu.ac.za/bitstream/e/10394/10458/No_68(2013)_Stemmet_J_&_Senekal_BA.pdf;jsessionid= 87486B5AD5 9 A0E81960B33 12BDF5E291?sequence=1

Tax Policy Center. (2020, May). *How do federal income tax rates work?* Tax Policy Center. https://www.taxpolicycenter.org/briefing-book/how-do-federal-income-tax-rates-work#:~:text=The%20rates%20apply%20to%20taxable

The Editors of Encyclopedia Britannica. (2018). Pacific War | Summary, Battles, Maps, & Casualties. In *Encyclopædia Britannica.* https://www.britannica.com/topic/Pacific-War

The Media Lab. (2019, November 5). *7 Key factors behind the success story of Netflix*. The Media Lab. https://www.themedialab.me/7-key-factors-behind-success-story-netflix/

The Novel Factory. (2022). *8 Proven Character Archetypes That Supercharge Your Story*. Novel Factory. https://www.novel-software.com/character-archetypes/#_Toc7000467

Tobias, A. (2022, April 22). *If You Can Solve These Puzzles, You May Be a Lateral Thinker*. PILGRIM SOUL CREATIVE. https://www.pilgrimsoul.com/home/if-you-can-solve-these-puzzles-you-may-be-a-lateral-thinker

Trafton, A. (2021, December 21). *Study finds a striking difference between neurons of humans and other mammals*. MIT News | Massachusetts Institute of Technology. https://news.mit.edu/2021/neurons-humans-mammals-1110

Tyatya, K. (2015, September 15). *"It takes a village to raise a child."* News24. https://www.news24.com/News24/it-takes-a-village-to-raise-a-child-20150921

UCL. (2020, August 3). *Energy demands limit our brains' information processing capacity*. UCL News. https://www.ucl.ac.uk/news/2020/aug/energy-demands-limit-our-brains-information-processing-capacity

Udemy. (2014, April 8). 7 Lateral Thinking Questions to Promote Out-of-the-Box Thinking. Udemy Blog. https://blog.udemy.com/lateral-thinking-questions/

University of Santa Barbra. (2019, September 16). *Differences in personality structure among humans*. ScienceDaily. https://www.sciencedaily.com/releases/2019/09/190916143945.htm

Usa.gov. (2018). *Top Questions About Social Security | USAGov*. Usa.gov. https://www.usa.gov/about-social-security

Vincent, J. (2020, February). *Buying vs. Leasing a Car*. U.S. News. https://cars.usnews.com/cars-trucks/advice/buying-vs-leasing

Waters, S. (2021, August 5). *The path to self-acceptance*. Www.betterup.com. https://www.betterup.com/blog/self-acceptance

WebMD. (2008, April 17). *Dissociative Identity Disorder (Multiple Personality Disorder)*. WebMD; WebMD. https://www.webmd.com/mental-health/dissociative-identity-disorder-multiple-personality-disorder

Weil cornel medicine. (2021, December 3). *Brain Drain: Scientists Explain Why Neurons Consume So Much Fuel Even When at Rest*. WCM Newsroom. https://news.weill.cornell.edu/news/2021/12/brain-drain-scientists-explain-why-neurons-consume-so-much-fuel-even-when-at-rest

Whelehan, B. (2022). *Estimated Tax Payments: How They Work And When To Pay Them*. Bankrate. https://www.bankrate.com/taxes/estimated-taxes/

Wong, K. (2012, August). *Why Humans Give Birth to Helpless Babies*. Scientific American Blog Network. https://blogs.scientificamerican.com/observations/why-humans-give-birth-to-helpless-babies/

Zadro, S. (2021, February 11). *Understanding your archetypal self*. WellBeing Magazine. https://www.wellbeing.com.au/mind-spirit/spirituality/jung-spiritual-archetype.html

Zelman, K. M. (2022). *Eat to Boost Your Energy*. WebMD. https://www.webmd.com/diet/obesity/features/eat-to-boost-your-energy#:~:text=Start%20off%20your%20new%20year

Zyga, L. (2008, November 13). *Study Shows How We Evolved Different Personalities*. Phys.org; Phys.org. https://phys.org/news/2008-11-evolved-personalities.html

## Image References

Spaniol, J. (2016). *Fighting for love*. Unsplash. [Image]. https://unsplash.com/photos/-L0N74GWsq8

Sikkema, K. (2019). *Editorial, Business & Work - Taxes*. Unsplash. [Image]. https://unsplash.com/photos/xoU52jUVUXA

papyonthemountain. (2017). *Volkswagon icecream truck*. Pixabay. [Image]. *https://pixabay.com/photos/vw-van-combi-retro-flightskwagen-2532708/*.

Tumisu. (2018). *Investment*. Pixabay. [Image]. https://pixabay.com/photos/investment-finance-time-3247252/